How to make an income from your art

Other titles from How To Books

LIKELY STORIES
*Fabulous, inspirational, chuckleworthy and deeply instructive tales about
creative writing as told to the author by his ubiquitous Guru*
HUGH SCOTT, Whitbread winning author

**HOW TO WRITE A CHILDREN'S PICTURE BOOK
– AND GET IT PUBLISHED**
ANDREA SHAVICK

HOW TO WRITE FOR TELEVISION
A guide to writing and selling successful TV scripts
WILLIAM SMETHURST

HOW TO WRITE GREAT SCREENPLAYS
And get them into production
LINDA JAMES

HOW TO WRITE YOUR FIRST NOVEL
SOPHIE KING

THE FIVE-MINUTE WRITER
Exercise and inspiration in creative writing in five minutes a day
MARGRET GERAGHTY

Write or phone for a catalogue to:

How To Books
Spring Hill House
Spring Hill Road
Begbroke
Oxford
OX5 1RX
Tel. 01865 375794

Or email: info@howtobooks.co.uk

Visit our website www.howtobooks.co.uk to find out
more about us and our books.

Like our Facebook page How To Books & Spring Hill

Follow us on Twitter @Howtobooksltd

Read our books online www.howto.co.uk

How to make

an income

from your art

Turn your *passion into profit* and thrive as an artist

ANN GADD

howtobooks

Published by How To Books Ltd
Spring Hill House, Spring Hill Road, Begbroke, Oxford OX5 1RX
Tel: (01865) 375794. Fax: (01865) 379162
info@howtobooks.co.uk
www.howtobooks.co.uk

How To Books greatly reduce the carbon footprint of their books by sourcing their typesetting
and printing in the UK.

British Library Cataloguing in Publication Data
A catalogue record for this book is available from the British Library

ISBN: 978 1 84528 494 7

Cover design by Baseline Arts, Oxford
Produced for How To Books by Deer Park Productions, Tavistock
Typeset by Kestrel Data, Exeter
Printed and bound in Great Britian by Bell & Bain Ltd, Glasgow

NOTE: The material contained in this book is set out in good faith for general guidance and
no liability can be accepted for loss or expense incurred as a result of relying in particular
circumstances on statements made in the book. The laws and regulations are complex and liable
to change, and readers should check the current position with the relevant authorities before
making personal arrangements.

To Anthony

We jumped off the cliff and, falling fearfully into the void . . .

found we could fly.

Other books by Ann Gadd:

Ewe at Work – Sheep Get Down to Business, Create Yourself Publications,
Cape Town (2012)

Lamb for Ewe? Create Yourself Publications, Cape Town (2011)

Wine a Bit and Ewe Will Feel Better, Gateway Publishing Limited, Sark (2011)

Making Your Art Work – A Guide to Making an Income from Art in South Africa,
Create Yourself Publications, Cape Town (2010)

What Went Wrong With Mr Right? Findhorn Press, UK (2009)

The Ambitious Sheep, Create Yourself Publications, Cape Town (2009)

The New Ewe, Create Yourself Publications, Cape Town (2007)

Climbing the Beanstalk – The Spiritual Truths in Fairy Tales, Findhorn Press,
UK (2007)

A–Z of Habits, Findhorn Press, UK (2007)

Life with Ewe, Create Yourself Publications, Cape Town (2007)

Finding Your Feet: How the Soles Mirror the Soul, Findhorn Press, UK (2006)

*The Girl Who Bites Her Nails and the Man Who Is Always Late: What Our Habits Reveal
About Us,* Findhorn Press, UK (2006)

Healing Habits, Kima Global, Cape Town (2003)

Contents

Creativity is another word for courage

Henri Matisse

Author's note

When, after a long career in advertising, my husband, Anthony, was forced to close his advertising agency, my world was thrown into disarray. More so because he announced cheerfully that he wanted to become an artist. Our residue savings from the company had been spent on a new (failed) venture. I was already an artist and had been so for eight years, juggling painting and conceptual art with freelance advertising, teaching art workshops, doing Reiki and giving alternative health treatments as well as writing books and articles.

We gave ourselves six months to see if we could make a viable living from art, remembering that we had two children to educate, a mortgage, and other expenses that went way beyond our own immediate needs. After five months I had exhausted myself in an attempt to keep the Gadd ship afloat and things weren't looking too hopeful. The couple of paintings I was selling a month, even with income from my other activities, was not sufficient.

Then, during the last month of the six-month trial period, Anthony's work started to sell. And, although I had painted sheep previously, I came up with the first 'sheep' painting in the style for which I have become known. While we don't exactly swan around in the latest 4×4s, we have been able to clothe, feed and provide a good education for our children, while at the same time enjoying a lifestyle which, given its freedom and creativity, many would aspire to.

This book is a personal experience of the art world. The information and experiences written about in this book may mirror your own, or you may find your path is very different. These insights are mine and, after requests to write about what I have learnt and the success I am enjoying as an artist, I have compiled this book, with the full understanding that no two journeys can be the same. Likewise I have attempted not to rate or judge one type of art, artist or gallery over another – artists are an extremely varied breed, from the Sunday blue-rinse brigade to the Steven Cohens of the world (sweeping the streets of the Heldenplatz in Vienna with a giant toothbrush, naked but for a corset, gas mask and high-heels). I cannot hope to have all the answers but, in writing this book, I hope to narrow the gap of understanding between artists and galleries, and what you need to do to be successful.

Names, in certain instances, have been changed to ensure anonymity.

Introduction

(Read this – it's important!)

Don't you wish sometimes that a fairy would come and wave a magic wand and make your life happen the way you want it to? That all those finished paintings or sculptures tucked at the back of your garage would be found by the curator of a famous art gallery and whisked away for a fortune and a bit of fame? Don't you long to win the art lotto and rise to the position of Picasso or Hockney? (Or even just the most well-renowned artist in your city?) Do you dream about making a living from art so that you can escape the drudgery of a job you lost interest in long ago? Do you feel confined, bored and depressed by the mundanity of your life and see being an artist as a way to find your true self?

This is the story of a man who found a fairy godmother who offered to change his life just the way he had dreamed.

An artist's (true) fairytale

Once upon a time there was a man who desperately wanted to be a full-time artist. He spent every day working in the business world, bemoaning the fact that he could not fulfil his dream. He blamed the world, his wife, the cat and life in general for his misfortune. He also wished that he wasn't so tired when he came back from work – too tired, in fact, to think about painting. If only he didn't have to spend so much time at work, and after work, doing chores and paying bills. He felt trapped by a large mortgage and the confines of his job. If only he was more inspired over the weekends to do something other than watch TV and drown his sorrows.

Years went by and the man became more angry and frustrated at not having his talent recognized, until one day a fairy godmother came into his life.

This fairy godmother had just inherited some cash – not a huge amount, but enough to feel she could help the man (who happened to be her boyfriend's brother). She took pity on him and decided to give him some money to help him with his predicament. She sat with him and discussed the problem at length. Finally, they worked out his expense budget for a year of mortgage repayments, electricity, food, petrol and so on until they reached a final amount required per month to live.

Then the fairy godmother said, 'I will give you this amount of money in a lump sum so that you can go and fulfil your dream of being an artist. You will have a year to achieve your dream, after which the calendar will strike 12 and you will be turned back into a hapless office worker if you have not found a way to turn your passion into a sustainable income'.

Whoosh! – She waved her magic cheque book and his city flat was rented, he'd moved to a small rural cottage, his suit changed into jeans and a T-shirt, his computer became a brush and canvas. And the cat? Well, the cat just stayed the same. Now the man looked and felt like an artist and he was ready to have a ball. This was IT. The break he had always wanted.

The first month was spent busily preparing his art space.

The second month was spent conceptualizing ideas for paintings.

In the third month, he started his first painting, which didn't really get finished until the fifth month, when he started on a series of works in earnest.

Three more months went by and he completed several paintings, but still had not earned a cent. He felt he needed more time before he could approach a gallery.

As the calendar threatened to strike 12, he had not been to a single gallery with his work. It was something he delayed and delayed until the twelfth month arrived and the fairy godmother, good as her word, refused to cough up any more cash.

Instantly, being cash-strapped, he was transformed back into a frustrated businessman. His studio became a corporate office, his palette and brush a computer, his jeans a rather shabby pair of chinos and he moved back into his flat. (The cat stayed on in the country, where he lived happily eating the mice that the fairy godmother had thankfully not turned into footmen.) As for the man, his dreams of living happily ever artist were destroyed and he was even more unhappy than before.

Moral of the tale:

You and you alone are responsible for fulfilling your dreams. You may have heaps of talent but without determination and discipline, your dream of making an income from art could be hard to transform into reality.

Only YOU can make your dreams happen. If you want to earn a living from art, you may experience a few lucky breaks along the way, but ultimately it's up to you to make it happen. In writing this book, it's my hope that I can pass on information, understanding and practical advice gained from my own journey, as well as those of a few other successful artists, so that you can turn your dream into reality.

1

Van Gogh in your psyche

There is a reason why 'pain' is found in the word '*pain*ting'. It's not that the actual process is necessarily painful (although it can be) – what creates pain for most artists is how to turn art into a viable income. You may love what you have created, but will the notoriously picky galleries feel the same? How will you move beyond mere survival to create a comfortable lifestyle? Mastering the art world is not just about mastering your chosen medium of expression.

There is a perception that becoming an artist is about opting out of 'real' life – it is a lifestyle desired by many, yet viewed as highly risky. It is the security of your uninspiring 9–5 job versus the freedom of doing what inspires you (with a bit of poverty thrown in for good measure). Many educators enhance this perception – rather than encouraging art as a career, they push students into alternative art-related careers such as graphic or product design, fashion, advertising or architecture.

Art degrees at universities seem to offer little in the way of practical issues such as marketing, PR or managing the financial and organizational aspects of your art business – all of which are key factors in ensuring success. Somehow, as artists, we believe that fame and fortune should just come knocking on our door; that we will one day be 'discovered' and won't have to get our hands dirty by dealing with the more mundane aspects of business, such as invoicing or following up on payments. Money is often viewed as a necessary evil – it has the power to create the lifestyle we desire, but we don't actually want to deal with it. And so we dream . . . and get disillusioned and bitter when nothing happens.

Van Gogh was reported as living in near poverty and dying with only one work sold. This concept of the tortured, penniless artist has seeped into our psyches, so that now we equate being an artist with being penniless. This may be true in some cases, but it is not *the* truth.

Artists in history: how the perception of the artist has altered through the ages

When people first scratched rudimentary depictions of the animals and gods who shared their world onto the walls of caves, they elevated themselves. Why? Because in recording tribal history or in predicting its future, they could do something unique and important. As their skills developed, their depictions became more accurate. Experimenting with different more permanent inks, the illustrations became a record of tribal life.

From these simple beginnings artists evolved who produced works of ever-increasing splendour and skill, and as a consequence they played a significant role in society. A reasonably good artist was assured of a relatively comfortable lifestyle in the Middle Ages and the Renaissance.

At what point did this change? When did artists stop being assured of a reasonable living, and where did the archetype of the anguished, impoverished artist arise?

I believe it started during the later part of the 19th century with movements such as impressionism, and developed later in the 20th century when artists rebelled against what they saw as bourgeois and colonial activities. Another object of their defiance was academia, the bastion of the art word. Art that conformed to the tastes of the bourgeois and academia was consequently challenged and resulted in movements such as Dadaism and expressionism.

In rebelling against the established patrons of art, artists lost their purchasers and, without this means of support, many became impoverished. By following their desire to create in a way that inspired them, they risked their potential to sell – and the idea of the artist starving for his/her art became embedded in society.

To some artists, the idea of living on the fringe of society and distancing oneself from its norms, creates a feeling of 'specialness'; the idea that simply by adopting the persona of the archetypal artist one has carved for oneself a unique place in history, irrespective of the quality of one's artistic work.

Today, we have adhered to the belief that being an artist gives one the privilege of living true to one's own passion and vocation at the expense of financial security. This archetype is Van Gogh's legacy (no offence to the poor man). The truth is that if you are to earn a good living from your art, then you must get rid of your Van Gogh complex.

Myths about artists

From wildly eccentric to plain boring, artists come in all shapes and sizes. Perhaps the common link is that we have had the courage to pursue a path that we are passionate about, instead of one dictated to by society. Because of this, artists are often seen as misfits who hover on the fringes. Yet, as Descartes says, 'most men lead lives of quiet desperation' because they are not following their hearts' desires, but a path they chose (or had chosen for them) when they were too young and uninformed to really know what they were getting into.

As the saying goes, 'if you're poor and don't conform, then you are seen as mad. If you're rich, you're seen as eccentric!'.

Insecure is the securest place to be: the myth of security

In the supposed 'good old days', provided you didn't arrive at work drunk (more than a few times), did a reasonable job (sometimes) and avoided groping the MD's PA (except at the annual Christmas bash), you were assured of a regular income and the occasional promotion. Big Daddy looked after his employees.

Then life moved into the fast lane. Mergers and acquisitions became the buzz words that haunted the corporate passages, creating fear and distrust among employees. Suddenly, the longer you had worked at a firm, the more of a liability you were.

Our ideas of security at the expense of our freedom no longer hold water: there are simply no guarantees. Corporate security can be an illusion and, paradoxically, being an artist can prove to be *more* secure. Being your own boss, you are responsible entirely for what you produce. There are no scapegoats, but there is also no one else making you the fall guy. This freedom naturally brings a great sense of joy and wellbeing.

Art as a business

I once walked into the offices of a powerful gallery owner. Michael owned seven galleries and as such could play a significant role in my career. A huge man with a mop of white hair, his booming voice only made him seem more intimidating to a nervous artist keen to make a good impression.

I had been summoned to the hallowed gallery HQ by a secretary and had dropped everything to be there, fearing that the opportunity would pass me by if I hesitated, even for a day. Now I was standing in one of his galleries, surrounded by some examples of my work, which had been hastily displayed around the room.

'Art, for me,' he said, 'is a business. Just that. Nothing personal or emotional in my decisions or transactions. Whether I like you or not is immaterial. I want to sell art and that is what drives my choices. I used to be in business,' he went on, 'until I got into the business of art. I believe my success has been because of this attitude.'

I was shocked. To me, a novice in the art world, art was about style, concept, passion, expression, beauty, mirroring our environment, emotion. In spite of my need to earn a living from art, business hadn't really entered my head. At that point, I believed that being an artist should preclude one from having to pay the rent; that good art should just sell itself. Arguing about pricing and financial transactions was simply not part of my reality. That was until Michael made an offer to purchase all the work I had available (admittedly at 25% less than I was asking for it). There and then, I was no longer an artist but a trader of sorts, earnestly attempting to get a better deal for my work.

As I drove home later, the deal concluded, I realized that art was not just about the fun aspect of creating – you have to have some business acumen for you to succeed. The encounter with Michael completely altered my perspective of the art world and I am extremely grateful to him for this awakening.

The artist archetype and how it affects you

The perception of an artist as being eccentric – as well financially and emotionally insecure – is one we often buy into when we decide to become a fulltime artist. Even if it is subconscious, we believe that if we dress funny, act irrationally and are irresponsible, somehow success must follow. This can have a profound effect on our ability to create a viable income.

Until you let go of the beliefs that say to be an artist means to struggle financially, be emotionally tortured, unstable and rejected by society, you will carry on perpetuating your belief.

How do you get rid of this belief? By first acknowledging that it is there.

How we buy into this belief

It was a PTA address to the final-year school leavers. Teachers took turns to stand up and speak about the different career opportunities linked to their particular subjects. The hall was packed as the headmaster, grinning enthusiastically, bounded onto the stage, while latecomers shuffled in surreptitiously through the side door, frantically switching their mobile phones to mute.

The learners fidgeted uncomfortably in their seats, wishing for the whole thing to be over so they could get home and start Facebooking or Twittering each other. Parents sat indulgently attempting to spot their offspring in the sea of blue blazers. The teachers, many of whom had never worked in the careers they were advocating, gave performances ranging from extremely uninspiring to well informed.

Then it was the turn of the art teacher who, dressed rather more flamboyantly than his colleagues, got up to speak.

'Making money from art is like this,' he addressed his audience. 'You like painting and listening to music, right?' There was a general murmur of assent from the pupils. 'Well, earning a living as an artist is just like earning a living from music. You may want to be a rock star. The reality, though, is that it's simply not possible, just as it's not possible to be an artist full time.'

I was stunned. In a few sentences he had filled these young and eager minds with the belief that art was not a possible career. It is this belief that had haunted me for years, and had forced me to stay in jobs I didn't enjoy.

To say I was angry was putting it mildly. I wanted to run onto the stage and tell the teacher how, in a single speech, he had destroyed the hopes of at least one budding young artist I knew was in the audience, and had perpetuated this belief for all the parents present. But, in fairness to the man, this had been *his* experience. *He* believed he couldn't make a living from art.

Throughout your childhood and adolescence, chances are that the seed of this belief was sown into your subconscious. And it is because of this inherent belief that most parents would be more thrilled to be told that their son or daughter wants to be a doctor than an artist.

One of the purposes of this book is to help you let go of that belief and replace it with one that serves your purpose better. Because *if you change the belief, then you change the outcome.*

Now ask yourself: is the idea that you can't make a living from art true? Or is it simply true because you say it's true?

Van Gogh and you

Some questions to ponder:

1. What artists do you know personally?
2. What sort of lives do they lead?
3. What inspires you about being an artist?
4. What do you fear most?
5. Is the fear based on experience or a belief you have made into a truth?

Exercise

Spend some time making a list of every successful living artist you know or have heard of. Do research, Google it, read *ARTnews*, *Modern Painters*, *Art Monthly* or any other art magazines you can find, but make that list as long as you can.

Then pin it up in a space where it's visible to you.

Add your name in bold to the list.

Now look at it and ask yourself, 'is it true that you can't make a living from art?' The proof that you can is literally staring you in the face. Ask yourself, 'Can I be on that list?' Then ask yourself, 'Why not?'

2

Working with the left side of your brain

An artist cannot fail; it is a success to be one.
~ Charles Horton Cooley

Everyone has talent. What is rare is the courage to follow the talent to the dark place where it leads.
~ Erica Jong

The art of self-expression

Sweaty palms, nervous coughing, procrastination, observing everyone else in the room, tentative light pencil, non-committal sketching and so on probably aptly describes how most of us act when confronted with a large white canvas and a paintbrush.

No matter how many paintings I do (over 4000 at last count, from the day I first put brush to canvas as a gangly schoolgirl), there is still something about a blank canvas that creates uncertainty, sometimes excitement and sometimes sheer terror. While we all have a strong desire to make our creative mark in life – be it in the kitchen, the garden or on stage, by creating a company or holding a paintbrush – many of us spend years avoiding whatever form our blank canvas takes, rather than risking failure.

9

But by avoiding failure, we also avoid success. One of the signs I used to hang on the wall at art workshops said, 'Paint as if you know you can't fail'. Then I would ask the participants to put on blindfolds, listen to music and paint with their left hands. In this situation they felt they could not succeed, so they could also not fail. That is the secret to your own creativity. And it's true – simply because to create *is* to succeed.

How many artists have failed to reach their potential because of fear, and how many artists have surpassed their potential and risen to great heights by overcoming their fear? Being creative takes courage. We have to put aside those nagging doubts that make us believe that we can fail and find the divinity within us that knows that failure is an illusion.

Everyone is a potential artist

> *Every child is an artist. The problem is how to remain an artist once we grow up.*
> ~ Pablo Picasso

We are all artists, yet somehow we have forgotten that along the way. There isn't a four-year-old around who believes he or she can't paint. As we've grown older, however, in most cases our education has done little to encourage our talents. In Chapter 4, I write about the left and right brain functions and how our general schooling system focuses heavily on the analytical left brain at the expense of the creative right brain. The result is that, by the age of 40, many people believe that they can't create.

What we refer to as God or the Divine is intrinsically creative. From the dinosaur to the dog, there has been a huge evolution and creative perfecting of the animal plan (T. rex, I suspect, seldom retrieved tennis balls!). The colour of flowers, the markings of insects, the evening sky – these are not signs of a Being who enjoys the dull and mundane. If the Divine is intrinsically creative, we as the micro-isms of that macro-ism must all be creative beings, yet many of us exist in lives of boring repetition. We do the same things, on the same days, at the same times – but in each and every one of us there is a small creative voice that begs to be heard. And we shut it down with the usual excuses: 'I'm too busy', 'I can't afford it', 'I don't know how' or 'I don't have the talent'.

When we do find the courage to explore our creativity, we engage with a magical process not dissimilar to the archetype of the magician or alchemist who can turn base metal into gold. When we are creative our inner 'magician' not only creates something to hang on the wall – through the transformation process, we are also transformed.

Art as your therapist

> *Every artist dips his brush in his own soul, and paints his own nature into his pictures.*
> ~ Henry Ward Beecher

> *Art is a step from what is obvious and well known toward what is arcane and concealed.*
> ~ Kahlil Gibran

> *The aim of art is to represent not the outward appearance of things, but their inward significance.*
> ~ Aristotle

When we create art, we explore our lives and the world around us. How we approach art is a mirror for how we live our lives. Our subject matter is a metaphor for the emotional issues that we are experiencing or have experienced in the past. By working with these issues, we not only feel more in control of the situation (we hold the paintbrush or creative direction), we also feel more empowered to change the picture to suit ourselves. By its nature, paint (particularly acrylic paint) dries quickly, allowing us to take away, paint over or add whatever else we desire. In so doing, we open the doors for change to manifest in our lives.

Often in our lives we are blinded to the very issues that most need our attention. Art is a wonderful tool for assisting us in the process of self-understanding. It becomes our mirror – something tangible that we can examine. Sometimes we may need the help of a facilitator to gently guide us to see and understand what eludes us. In letting go of draining emotional issues, we also become less burdened and stressed and therefore more able to cope with the changes that occur in our lives.

A lovely example is a painting by an art workshop participant of a wheelbarrow filled with gardening tools and surrounded by a large, imposing fence. During the workshop she spoke of the many changes she wanted to make in her life but felt unable to because she felt she lacked the appropriate tools. This left her feeling frustrated and unfulfilled. Through her painting, her subconscious mind conveyed the message that she had all the tools she needed – she simply had to find a way to access them. After realizing this, she changed her painting by adding a gate. Now that she could access the wheelbarrow and the tools, she could open up the possibility of accessing her own hidden talents so that she could make the changes she wanted to make. By constructing our reality in a painting, we are empowered to be more in control of our own lives.

What we suppress also gets expressed through our art. Unconsciously or consciously, when we create, we engage with that which is concealed within us – images spring from the subconscious into a conscious form. The concept becomes a visible representation of our emotions and thoughts, which we can explore, transform and ultimately release.

Art is a great way of releasing emotions because it is a visible (as opposed to verbal) medium and therefore more tangible. It also allows for change – you can paint over the bits that no longer please or serve you. This is a tremendously empowering process, more so because *your* free will is controlling the journey.

During the eight years that I held art workshops, there was seldom a day when at least one person did not become very emotional and, in doing so, release some old emotional baggage through the process of painting. So, if you want to shift some issues, turn off the TV and pick up a brush! Explore, have fun, express and engage with creativity – and, in the words of William Wordsworth, 'fill your paper with the breathings of your heart'. Give yourself the artistic licence to do so!

Approaching your creativity as a journey, not a goal

There are two ways to create:

- The left-brain way is to set a goal and then attempt to achieve it.

- The right-brain way starts out with no clear direction, using intuition as a guide. It is a way of doing something because it feels right. We don't think, 'In *The Artists' Book of Oil Painting* it says I should use blue next to orange to get a bright contrast' – we just feel that it may be interesting to see this divine blue just there next to the sensual burnt orange.

When I first started to paint, I set goals: I had already visualized the complete picture before I'd begin, so painting was simply the laborious process of achieving the desired result. Now, while I may start with an initial idea, I allow that idea to change and evolve as I paint. I allow myself to *feel* the painting as opposed to *thinking* about what should go where. It was through this more playful approach that the 'sheep' evolved for which I have become known.

As a result of this process, I no longer controlled the painting as much as flowed with it. In a sense, it became effortless. The same can be said for horse riding, golf, dancing or any other sport or artistic pursuit – when we connect with our centre, creativity flows naturally. It comes from a sense of *knowing* we can do it, rather than hoping that we can. I have seen people who have never put brush to paper produce works of great beauty using this approach.

How we express ourselves creatively mirrors how we live our lives. If we paint small, timid brushstrokes in one corner of our painting, we might need to ask ourselves whether we feel small and timid. By finding the courage to explore our art in different forms we can change different aspects of ourselves.

The creative block

At times you may run into a creative block. A period when fresh ideas just won't surface; when what seemed easy before now becomes laborious and doesn't work; a time when fear creeps into your psyche, whispering, 'was that my last good work? Am I destined to be no better? Am I a one-hit wonder who will fade into obscurity?'

I have walked into this quagmire. At my deepest moment of despair, when I was crying tears of anger, frustration and helplessness, a creative idea came to me. Now I have learnt to accept that all things are cyclical. We can't live in a state of constant creation 24/7. Cycles require periods of growth and expansion, and periods of consolidation and contraction. We each have our own seasons of autumn, winter, spring and summer. Fighting against this is like attempting to keep a cloud in the same position in the sky, or hold back the tide.

Acceptance of these cycles brings a kind of peace. In time, when I felt the Creative Block taking hold, instead of panicking, I left my art for a while and threw myself into something more mundane – something I could already do, such as cleaning a cupboard or painting a bedroom.

Often when we believe we are failing, it is our ego who is in charge, either telling us we are useless or over-inflating our accomplishments to our own detriment (like convincing us that our unimaginative or technically lacking art is brilliant). It's my belief that we block our creativity when we allow our egos to take over the process, rather than becoming a channel through which ideas and creativity flow.

Doing something more ordinary has a double benefit – it quietens our ego, which can neither boost nor belittle us, and through achieving something relatively easy (even if it's only a well-painted house or a tidy studio), it gives us a sense of accomplishment. And that's just what we need to give us the courage to get creating again.

Much of the interior of my house was painted in this wintery stage of creation. Somehow, doing practical tasks reduced my angst and I felt a real sense of achievement when the walls sparkled with their new paint. At other times, I'd tidy up instead of forcing a process that wasn't working. At some point the desire to create would spark again and I'd head back to the studio, revitalized and ready to start my creative spring.

Change as a mantra

When you have found your signature style – when you have an art form that is recognizably yours and does not prompt people to compare it to other artists – then you are well on the road to success. Imagine now that you've started enjoying some of the fruits of your labour. Money is coming in; art is leaving your studio.

Why change? One successful artist I know makes a discipline of reinventing herself every winter when sales are quiet. This takes courage, yet unless you keep looking at what you do in a different way, you threaten to become stagnant.

I have tried many new styles and approaches. Mostly I come back to the style I am best known for, but the exploration keeps me fresh and ready to move on when the time arises. If I stop exploring, then maybe some time down the road I'll be afraid to.

Art is like any exercise – to keep fit, you need to put in hours of training. When I stopped painting for nine despondent months at one stage, it took me a long time to get art-fit again and rebuild my confidence. I won't make that mistake again. Allow yourself a day, a week or a week every two months to explore and play beyond your style and comfort zone.

Finding a balance between art and life

Because society is more traditionally patriarchal (although this is changing), we tend to put emphasis and value on 'doing', which is related to the masculine principle, rather than 'being', which relates to the female principle.

One of the many things I have learnt as an artist is the value of being. Standing back and looking at your work can be as important as actually creating it. You may see things that you would otherwise have missed. (Looking at your work in a mirror or upside down is a great way to get a fresh take on it.) It is part of the male aspect to be 'out there', creating what we anticipate will meet the expectations of others. We become so focused on achieving our goals that we forget to enjoy the journey.

This lesson extends further into our lives in general. We tend to put our life and enjoyment on hold until we feel we've made it. This is like people living for the day they will retire (only to drop dead a week after they've got their gold watch). So live each moment of your artistic life. Balance doing with being – too much of one will create imbalance and unhappiness.

Getting your subconscious to enhance your goals

After I got over my teenage fantasies of being a rock star, I decided I wanted to write and paint for a living. Becoming an advertising art director and writing for magazines became my way of fulfilling my dreams. Problem was, it didn't. Designing adverts for others, often for products that did not inspire me, and writing articles about boardsailing competition results, didn't feel the way I had expected it to feel. Often when we are afraid to engage with the career choice we really want, we pick something close to it, so we have the copywriter who wants to be an author, or the gallery owner who had dreams of being an artist. We keep feeling like we are nearly there – close, but not close enough.

Having a definite goal helps us focus more on the goal and less on the fear of achieving it. And your goal will be easier to achieve if you harness the power of your subconscious. Here is an exercise that will help you define your goal of being an artist.

Exercise

1) Write down at least 20 reasons why you want to be an artist.

2) Then write down what attributes you have as an artist.

3) Now write down any blocks you feel may be stopping you.

4) Spend time with each block and write down ways you can address each issue. Don't stop until you've found a creative solution for each block (even if it's off the wall!).

The following exercise will introduce your goal to your subconscious to the process of transformation you want to go through.

17

Exercise

1) Get a large canvas or sheet of paper and book yourself off for at least six hours.

2) Start by painting/drawing/doodling your life as it is now.

3) On the same paper/canvas add images of your life/self as you would like to it to be.

4) Paint a studio, clients, your desired surroundings, money or anything that you desire.

5) Once you feel you have finished, paint over the things that you want to let go of. Change and rework things until you like what you see. Don't stop before then.

6) Take time to reflect on what you chose to let go of and what you saw as important to living your dream life.

Sounds wacky? Not so. Art is about creating. Before we can get what we want, we need to visualize what it is we want. The more definite we are about what we want, the easier it manifests. Numerous statistics show that students who monitor their goals by writing them down and keeping check of their progress are far more likely to be successful. By actually painting your goal you add a further dimension to the process. You make it real.

The book and movie *The Secret* explains that painting is a great way to make our dreams a reality. This simple process starts a communication about your desires with your subconscious (which, indecently, relates far better to visual images than written ones). Having made it real on your canvas, you push the start button to create that reality in your life.

The following exercise will help you create a logo that symbolizes what you want for yourself. Artists respond well to visual images, so having a logo to constantly remind you of your focus is a way of creatively harnessing your subconscious mind.

Exercise

First, identify the things you desire and draw them simply. In this case, it's a brush for painting, a frame for the artwork and a money bag for an abundant income!

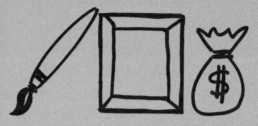

Figure 2.1

Now simplify them even further. I have done a 'P' (Figure 2.2) for the act of painting, a frame for the end artwork and a dollar sign.

Figure 2.2

Combine them into a single image or logo (Figure 2.3)

Figure 2.3

This now becomes your logo, which incorporates those things that you want. The simpler the final logo, the better. (It's not important if all your initial symbols are not visible – your subconscious will know what it stands for.)

Lastly, put it somewhere where you will be constantly reminded of your goal – such as the ceiling above your bed, the wall opposite where you work, or the fridge. Or have several in different places. Each time you look at the logo, you will be reinforcing your goals to your subconscious mind – this is incredibly powerful and can make just about anything happen.

Figures 2.4, 2.5 and 2.6 contain another example of this.

(1)   (2)   (3)

Figure 2.4

The symbols illustrate my intention: (1) I (2) support my family (3) through art.

(1)   (2)   (3)

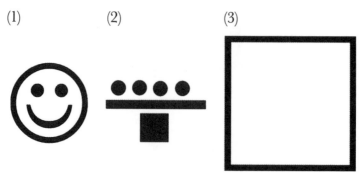

Figure 2.5

The smiley face in Figure 2.5 represents me being happy having achieved the goal, the next illustration represents support for me, while the box is a simplified frame, symbolizing a painting. I combined them into a logo (Figure 2.6).

Figure 2.6

This example was from artist Stephen Parsons.

Figure 2.7

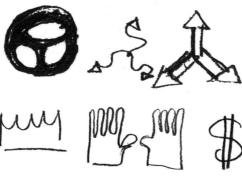

Figure 2.8

21

Figure 2.9

You may start thinking that I've lost the plot here, but truly your subconscious mind responds to symbols, and it's your subconscious mind that you need to engage with if you are to be successful. If you don't have its buy-in, your chances of success are radically reduced.

A story about the power of visualization

A woman came to an art workshop I was giving. During the day she painted a small cottage next to a river against a backdrop of mountains. She explained that, having recently got divorced, she was not in a good space, and that the picture represented the peace that she was seeking. A few months later I received an email asking me to change her email address because she was emigrating to New Zealand. When she contacted me next, it was to say that her sister had found her a cottage to rent and the weird thing was that the cottage and the setting were almost exactly as she had painted them months ago. And, she added, she was now finding the peace she had been seeking.

After teaching art workshops for eight years, I have heard many such stories. From finding a partner to creating a new lifestyle, this exercise can have incredibly powerful results.

3

Ten blocks to creativity

'I'd love to, but I can't right now'

The more I come to understand about the nature of creativity, the more I see the artist not just as the person who creates images. Rather, in the broadest sense, the artist has the potential to create the life that he or she wants, because life is the ultimate creation. Creating is much more than what we do – it is how we live our lives.

Blocks and breakthroughs

The universe is in a constant process of creation and destruction. Each new day brings with it the inevitability of nightfall. Each flower blooms only to shrivel and die. We too are consciously or unconsciously involved in the act of creating or destroying. When we initiate something, whether it's a painting, a garden or a piece of prose, we are in tune with the universe and feel connected to its rhythm. In this state, we can soar above our worldly trials to capture moments of extreme bliss and passion. This is the delicious reward for flowing with our creativity – it is the essential nature of life. When we pursue addictions, sabotage our success or stay in destructive relationships, we hold ourselves back from becoming all we are capable of being.

If engaging with our artistic skills can bring such fulfilment, why do we so often avoid it? We keep meaning to get to it, but other things seem to keep coming up. We create blockages rather than breakthroughs.

Does one of these scenarios sound like you?

- Your 9-to-5 job is getting you down and you are counting the days to retirement when life will really start. You have an idea that you want to explore your artistic potential and, if possible, make it financially viable. Although you just can't seem to get down to doing any painting now, you have done some sums to see what kind of income you would need to make from your art if you took early retirement.

- You find yourself unemployed and at last have time to do your own thing, which in your case is painting. But months have gone by and the same old canvas is still sitting on your easel. Your partner keeps nagging you to do something but you just don't feel motivated.

- The children have left home and you finally have time on your hands now that you aren't lifting, cooking and caring. You miss them hugely, but have been looking forward to finding out who you really are by exploring your talents. When you were knee-deep in washing you always imagined having this time, but now it's here, you just haven't really been inspired to create.

- You've just come out of art school and are keen to be independent. However, you find that without deadlines, the inspiration from lecturers and the camaraderie of being with other students, you don't feel motivated to be creative. This makes you feel guilty and insecure, which makes it even harder to face that white canvas.

Why is this happening?

You may have had this dream for your whole life, yet when the opportunity to fulfil it arrives, you find all sorts of reasons for why you are not able to. In my own work as well as that of my art workshop participants, I have come to identify ten major blocks which affect us all to a greater or lesser extent. Knowing what these blocks are and being able to identify where your own energy gets stuck will help you to break through them.

1. The 'having no time' block

'I just don't have the time,' we say as we fumble for the TV remote or have another glass of wine.

Most people say that they don't have time for themselves. I recall a retired man who was constantly telling me that he didn't have time to paint. When I enquired as to what exactly was filling his time, he mentioned things like answering emails, reading the newspaper, having drinks with friends. When we are afraid to explore our creativity, we will fill our lives with pastimes to convince ourselves that it's not our fault we are not painting. There are always just so many other things that have to be done.

If we are employed or have a family (or both!), we may genuinely struggle to fit our artistic interests into an already hectic schedule. Many of us become adept at putting our own needs at the bottom of the pile. Often, would-be artists end up feeling frustrated and resentful towards others who they see as standing in the way of their creative ambitions.

If, in order to maintain our lifestyle, we get up at the same time, dress in the same order, perform the same ablutions, and drive through the same traffic to perform the same routine tasks, day after day, it is not surprising that much of our creative potential becomes stifled. We simply don't have energy at the end of the day to be creative – any time we have to spare is spent recuperating.

So how we can create time to pursue our artistic interests? This is where discipline comes into play. Setting aside a few hours a week, which are non-negotiable, will go a long way to rejuvenating you and allowing you to function more effectively in your life. Doing so will also lessen frustration and resentment which will have been adding to your stress levels.

In the book *The Artist's Way*, Julia Cameron (2011) explains in detail why setting up this 'me' time is so essential to our well-being. Each time we create something we expand and nurture our potential artist.

2. The 'not having the skills/knowledge' block

'I *want* to be an artist,' you may say, 'but I didn't go to art school and don't have the qualifications. Someone with training will have a huge advantage over me so it's not even worth trying. Until I have done any number of art courses and bought any number of 'how to' books and practised any number of techniques, I will be wasting my time.' It's no wonder that this type of thinking stifles our ability to create!

Many years ago I attended an art class with a woman who had already got a degree in fine art. She wanted to become a full-time artist, she told me, but didn't feel qualified enough. So she was taking art classes at the same time as doing her masters in art through correspondence. Only after she had completed her masters, and perhaps studied under a great artist in Europe, did she feel she would be sufficiently qualified. I was amazed that she believed that the more qualifications she achieved the better artist she would be. As if study in art was a guarantee for success!

Fact: *formal training does not guarantee you a higher income – in fact, it doesn't guarantee you one at all!*

Art is one of the few careers where formal training is not a prerequisite and does not guarantee success. (I'm not saying that qualifications aren't beneficial – just that they're not essential.)

As children, we learn that to move to the next grade we need to study and pass an exam. As adults we continue to believe that the more art education we receive, the better artist we will be. And without it, we don't feel we *qualify* to create. But do we really need lessons on self-expression?

Formal training can, in fact, be rather inhibiting in that it teaches you 'the rules'. Take the case of an art teacher who asked to come and visit our studio. She confessed to being very envious of our situation as she had always wanted to paint rather than teach. Formally trained, she regaled in horror when she saw the vast array of different media Anthony was using in his work (he likes experimenting!). 'But you can't use that!' was her reaction, 'these aren't the materials artists are supposed to use'.

We can learn a lot from children. A three-year-old takes immense pleasure in creating. He or she explores the potential of their creative tools without worrying about composition, history, perspective or what technique to use. Paint is bright and squishy and follows your fingers magically on a page. Both hands are double the fun, especially when the colours squelch into one another. It's also brilliant to mush your hands into mud and then smear it on the pavement in patterns, or paint war masks on faces ripe with the juice of ripe mulberries. Young children create naturally and spontaneously – it's about letting go of your expectations and enjoying it.

Let go of the belief that you have to have formal training to explore your art. Toulouse-Lautrec, Paul Gauguin and Vincent Van Gogh didn't, so it shouldn't stop *you*!

3. The 'having no space' block

'I've wanted to paint for years, but I'll have to wait until my daughter leaves home/we can afford to renovate/I move out of digs/we buy a bigger place. Then, once I have a studio, I'll start.' Sounds familiar?

A man I knew constantly used the lack of space as an excuse for not painting. Finally his wife relented and the study became the studio. An easel was purchased, as well as top-quality paints and brushes, a comfortable stool and all the other equipment he required. Did he paint? Occasionally. But by then the conversation had changed to not having enough *time* to paint. The truth is, he was afraid of exploring his art in case he was 'not good enough'. Creating blockages was his way of avoiding these uncomfortable feelings.

When we really want to paint, we will create a space – any space. I have seen established artists use their bedrooms, the garage or the kitchen table to produce their work. One husband and wife I taught used the roof space in their small duplex. You couldn't stand up and it could get hellishly hot – but they were so busy painting they didn't notice!

We can adapt even the smallest area in a house or apartment into a workroom. In fact, the whole world can become our studio – try painting outdoors! Be creative in how you adapt to your situation, and remember that when you allow yourself the *emotional space* to create, the physical space will follow.

A few years ago, after becoming too cramped in our shared 'office', Anthony and I built a studio so that we would have more space to paint. It was just bigger than a single garage. Within six months Anthony had started working on larger works, several at one time, so it was too small. We relocated to our double garage and the cars stayed outside. A year later, with our paintings selling well, we found this space too small as well, so we bought a house to use as a studio. It wasn't six weeks later that we had to have a 6×4-metre wooden room delivered, just to accommodate the finished works before they went off to galleries. If the initial lack of space had put us off, we would never have started the journey.

4. The 'can't afford it' block

'When I can afford the paints/brushes/canvases, then I'll be able to paint.' How often do we say we lack the appropriate equipment and can't afford to buy what we need? While the aficionados of the formal art world may frown upon ordinary acrylic PVA or enamel paint, many top artists I know use unconventional paints, even if it's only to 'kill' the canvas before applying more expensive materials. Ordinary paint products have developed dramatically over the past few years and their ability to withstand fading has improved greatly.

Likewise with brushes – I long ago gave up the need to use sable-hair brushes and other expensive tools (this way, I avoid feeling bad when I forget to wash them). It's a relief to be able to toss out a brush that's losing hair or dried hard with paint, knowing that it hasn't cost you the earth.

At a Marlene Dumas exhibition I was surprised to see that she often doesn't stretch her watercolour paper, while at an exhibition of William Kentridge's I saw that many of his initial drawings were done on what appeared to be newsprint.

It may not be the way to impress a gallery (until you are established enough to be able to paint on whatever you want!), but as a start, these kinds of measures will allow you to explore your art and not count the cost!

5. The 'perfection' block

'I'll take the plunge when I can be assured that I can paint perfectly.'

There's a bit of a perfectionist lurking in most of us. When we start out painting we all have a desire to produce the perfect work. Yet it is often the very imperfection of a work that makes it appealing, just as it is often when we let go of the need for perfectionism that the artist within us emerges.

I have seen any number of artists laboriously attempting to paint a realistic version of a subject only to end up frustrated and disheartened. When we have fixed ideas about how one should paint, or about what art is, we can become so caught up in proving ourselves correct that we disconnect ourselves from the joy of creating. (People with these issues often propel themselves into art-administration positions, where they are able to 'control' other artists and direct the way art should be.)

Perfectionism restricts rather than frees our creativity. Besides, what is perfect? At a recent Biennale I walked around with two other artists and viewed the work of over 800 artists from different corners of the world. What one of us thought was brilliant barely raised interest in the others. Is Picasso more perfect than Pissarro? Is Warhol perfect while Manet falls short? Who is to say? What is the perfect painting? Ask 20 different artists or art dealers and you'll get 20 different replies.

There is no right or wrong in art. We need to find the courage to let go, loosen up and just see what will happen – and if it works for you, then it works. At the same time, one accepts that it may well not work for someone else. And that's OK.

If you're still hung up on creating 'perfect' work, look at it this way: does perfectionism denote completion? Is a closed bud more perfect than the open flower? A baby more beautiful than a child? Yet, we have come to believe that something can't be perfect if it's not complete. But nothing in the universe is complete – everything is in the process of growth or decay. From this perspective then, everything is imperfect as it changes and alters, or everything is perfect – always (the bud and the flower, the baby and the child – and the adult too!). And that includes your art. So stop seeking perfection – it already is!

6. The 'approval' block

'I will only start painting if I know that all my relations/friends/colleagues/galleries are going to love my work.'

We are so adept at judging what we create. And we are so quick to belittle ourselves and our creativity, and affirm our failures. Haven't you described yourself as 'useless' when it comes to art/baking/dancing/singing? Perhaps someone passed that comment to you as a child and it's remained tucked away in your subconscious. Perhaps every time you do something creative there's a voice telling you what you are doing is foolish and not good enough.

Perhaps the way you describe your art has something in common with the way you feel about yourself?

Here's an exercise that might surprise you:

Exercise
Get an elastic band and put it on your wrist. Every time you find yourself judging yourself or someone else, give it a good twang. By the end of the day, if your wrist is red you'll realize just how much energy you spend judging.

We are often our own worst enemies and bring ourselves down long before others are critical of us. I remember a friend asking me why I always belittled my achievements. It shocked me – I was not aware I was doing that. Then I started keeping score, and sure enough I never missed an opportunity. I didn't need anyone else to make me feel bad – I was doing a great job of it already! This awareness was profound and made me reconsider many aspects of my life. I realized that part of the reason I was making myself small was that I was afraid that I'd lose my friends, that they'd see my success as a threat. Sounds crazy, right? But many of us do this – we believe that to stand out means to stand alone. So we belittle ourselves in order to belong.

You've no doubt heard the following words from Nelson Mandela's 1994 inauguration speech (written by Marianne Williamson), but they are extremely relevant to your goal of being a full-time artist. So here is a reminder:

> *Our deepest fear is not that we are inadequate.*
> *Our deepest fear is that we are powerful beyond measure.*
> *It is our light, not our darkness, that frightens us.*
> *We ask ourselves, who am I to be brilliant, gorgeous, talented and fabulous?*
> *Actually, who are you not to be?*

You are a child of God.
Your playing small doesn't serve the world.
There's nothing enlightened about shrinking
So that other people won't feel insecure around you.

During the art workshops I run, we work with creating a non-judgmental space. Laughing at how we judge ourselves goes a long way towards releasing the need to do so. The following exercise always creates laughter:

Exercise

Write down a list of your achievements. All of them – from winning a prize at school to helping a friend in need. Acknowledge all that you have done. Pin it up somewhere visible so that whenever you are feeling small you can look at it. Add to it daily. Doing so will help you believe in your own self-worth.

We waste so much energy in life being concerned about what other people think. It starts with seeking the approval of our parents and ends with seeking approval from the rest of the world – from bosses to buddies, the people in the supermarket to the people who share our bedroom, the list is endless. And most of us become slaves, at least at some time in our lives (but often all the time), to the approval of others. Why? Because deep down we don't approve of ourselves.

Transfer this to our art and what happens? We seek the approval of gallery owners, critics, mothers, uncles, cousins, colleagues and our children for our art. We are desperate to hear those magic words, 'Gee, that's really great'.

Of course it's not wrong to want to hear those words. It's perfectly natural. But when we focus more on other people's approval than on the work itself, when we modify our work and second-guess what others might like, that is when we lose our sense of self. When we paint for others' approval, a part of ourselves begins to resent them for manipulating and controlling what we do. This can be mild, but it can build up until we are seriously angry at ourselves for pleasing others at the expense of pleasing ourselves.

It is draining to work on something while focusing on what others will think – and this is energy that could be going into our work. We also tend to paint smaller, tighter and more controlled work when we paint for others. I see this in children. Give a three-year-old some paint and paper and the chances are the paper will be filled with large, bold images. As children get older, the boldness and size of their work decreases; by their teenage years, many will start in a small corner, barely making an impression. Why? Because in their delight of the sensual mess of paint, paper and brush, the three-year-old has no need for approval. As children mature, the need for approval increases, particularly from their peers, and their work becomes increasingly inhibited. Seeking external approval inhibits your self-expression.

7. The 'domination' block

'If I can't be the best, then I won't paint.' If we have a huge fear of not being 'the best' – of not winning everything we enter – we may not do many of the things we want to do. If my fear of failure is greater than my desire to succeed, then opting out often seems like the best option.

A woman once told me, 'I always wanted to paint and did some painting at home. Finally I was persuaded to go to a painting class. I left after two weeks though. The others were much more advanced than I was; I didn't feel comfortable being there'.

If we put so much energy into assessing whether we are better or worse than every other artist, we inhibit our ability to create. The need to always be the best comes at the expense of your creative energy. More often than not in my art workshops, it was the official 'artists' who were straining trying to live up to their own expectations.

8. The 'security' block

Maybe you are convinced that the world and everyone in it is set on copying your idea/style. You become paranoid about this belief to the point that you use it as a reason for not taking your work to galleries, festivals or exhibitions. You may mask this insecurity with arrogance, at the same time over-inflating your history and achievements.

In your desire to achieve, anyone else who is successful is 'The Enemy'. You downgrade their achievements and caustically criticize their work, believing that there are only just so many pieces of the success pie to go around. (In fact, you wish they'd choke on their piece of pie.)

There is no limit on the number of artists who can succeed. Someone else's success has no doubt come about through discipline, courage, creativity and talent – so even if you don't appreciate their work, acknowledge the other elements of their success. Don't allow yourself to slip into this destructive, ungracious thinking. Curators don't want to know your biased opinion of their exhibition selection and how much better yours is. Creating negativity is not going to help your career. Rising above it and enjoying others' successes opens the door to your own.

In the book *Spiritual Capital*, Dan Zohar and Ian Marshall (2004) have created a 'Scale of Motivations' rated from −8 to +8 (a similar one is found in *Power vs Force* by David R. Hawkins). We move up and down this scale according to our state of being: at the highest level of +8 we reach enlightenment, while at the lowest level we are in a state of depersonalization (a state defined as 'an empty shell, with no core'). Such a state would define burnt-out alcoholics and drug addicts who have lost all hope of recovery.

Some artists find themselves in this position. I heard of a popular artist who weaned himself off drugs just to plunge heavily into alcohol and who now can't paint because his hands shake too much. It's a helpless and, in many cases, a hopeless position. Why am I telling you this? If we examine Zohar and Marshall's chart, we find that the pole of Exploration (+1) covers 'curiosity, the desire to explore and a sense of wonder', traits which are usually found in those interested in artistic pursuits. Opposite this pole is Self-assertion (−1), which is associated with 'thoughtlessness, unbridled competitiveness, too much pride, self-centredness and aggression . . . they are driven by a need for status and self-esteem of a sort dependent on others'.

What this is saying is that the latter type of behaviour precludes the former: energy that goes into manipulating and destroying other artists is the shadow side of ourselves, and denies your own exploration and creativity. Entertaining the negative destroys the positive.

Higher up the scale at +5 we find 'Generativity'. This is defined as: 'a special manifestation of creativity. It is creativity driven by love or passion'. This is when your art is your passion – you create because it is essential to your being. It gives one a sense of: 'playfulness about their creativity. The work is the life. Because creativity is so closely linked to play, generative people . . . are excited by anything that arouses their interest or creativity'. On the opposite end of the scale there is 'Anguish': 'a sense of loss or helplessness to decide what to do. The generative process is blocked. We feel stuck'.

Can you see how the more we stay in the negative aspect, the more we hold back on experiencing its opposite? Experiencing creativity and the joy of creating means letting go of angst, fear, craving and anger.

The opposite of construct is destruct. If we're not creating, then we might be destroying (ourselves or others.)

9. The 'blaming/shaming' block

Artists are notorious for having excuses for why they are not working. They are 'conceptualizing', 'uninspired' or they 'can't find the right reference'. When, at the end of the month, we have little or no work completed (and no money in the bank), we shift into guilt mode.

This is not a fun place to be, so the next step is to find someone or something to blame. This anger towards ourselves for not being and doing what we aspire to be and do (unless you are fairly self-actualized) will turn outwards into anger towards others. Gallery owners, other artists and/or your partner – all may fall victim to your attacks, as well as anyone who you see as having achieved their goals in life. Your creativity and your career as an artist has become the vehicle by which you express your frustration and anger. Your art is destructive as opposed to constructive.

10. The 'rules' block

I regularly receive an emailed newsletter from someone in the art retail world. Aside from understandably promoting certain products, it often describes what's 'right' and what's 'wrong' in terms of materials, style, and so on. If artists were still painting according to the rules established by the old masters 300 years ago, we'd have missed out on impressionism, pop art, surrealism, expressionism and performance art, to name just a few.

Artists have always pushed the boundaries in style, materials and subjects. Why would you not want to? So learn the rules by all means, and then have a lot of fun breaking them. Although I'll say it again: you don't need to know all the rules before you can start creating (in fact, you don't even have to know any).

Why we really create these blocks

All of these blocks have one thing in common: *fear.*

Creating is often more terrifying than we care to admit. The fear is that we will be judged 'not good enough'; that our art will be rejected; that what we create will not meet with the approval of ourselves or of others. Rather than experiencing this feeling of inadequacy, it becomes easier to shut ourselves off from our artistic nature and return to the safety of more mundane chores.

It took years before I could call myself an artist. When asked, I would mumble, 'Well, I paint sometimes'. Owning the label 'artist' was awesome and I was afraid that if I called myself an artist, I would set myself up for an inevitable tumble. It seemed easier to avoid the title so that no one could say I wasn't good enough to be one. Because I felt small, I painted small (and sold small as well).

Fear constricts controls and diminishes. Or it manifests as an over-inflated sense of self and the need to manipulate and dominate over others. We will create blocks as long as we are afraid to put ourselves 'out there' and accept that in order to succeed we may need to fail a few times along the way.

Fear also projects us into the future. We fear what will happen to us if we don't have enough money one day. We fear what others will think of us. We might be afraid of a journey we have to take. But it's important to realize that *none of the events that create fear have actually happened yet.*

We become so obsessed with trying to control the future that we forget to be in the now. Books such as Eckhard Tolle's incredible *The Power of Now* (2001) teach us the value of being present. It is, in fact, the only place where we can find true peace and joy. On either side of it we struggle to forgive ourselves for past mistakes or we worry about future failures.

I believe great art comes from being fully present, when 100% of your energy is focused on the work – not on the kids, the client who hasn't paid, your partner or the mortgage. A life-coach friend of mine put it well when she said, 'Acknowledge your fear and act in spite of it'. It's a case of saying, 'OK, I'm afraid of messing up this large canvas I've just bought, but I'll tuck the fear under my arm and paint anyway'.

It is only by focusing on the extreme joy of the creative moment that we can truly experience our connectedness to the universe. In this space there is no fear, only the sheer, unadulterated bliss of creating, no matter what the outcome. If you find yourself creating the blocks listed in this chapter, understand that it is your fear emerging.

4

Using our left or right brain functions

We all use both our left and right brain functions, although most often – depending on our age, education, environment and general life experience – one side is more dominant.

> *Right-brain thinking is*: random, intuitive, holistic, synthesizing, creative, subjective, 'big picture' view, emotional, imaginative, symbols and images, present and future, philosophy and religion, spatial perception, knows object function, fantasy based, presents possibilities, impetuous, risk taking.

> *Left-brain thinking is*: logical, sequential, rational, analytical, objective, focused on individual parts, words and language, present and past, maths and science, able to comprehend, knowing, acknowledging, order/pattern perception, knows object name, reality based, strategic, practical, safe.

Before going to school, which is traditionally geared to more left-brain thinking (logic, languages, practicality, conformity, analytical thinking), most children are predominately right brained. Sadly, by the time they are seven years old, only 10% of these children will still be classified as highly creative, and by adulthood this will have dropped to only 2%. Research is showing that people with optimum mental ability use both sides of their brains together – this may be the key to superior intellectual abilities.

As an artist, chances are that you would be more right brained (although not always). You'll experience a degree of resistance towards this chapter because the exercises are more analytical (left brained) in nature. They won't feel like fun and, unless you are very disciplined, you'll probably convince yourself that they are completely unnecessary.

But like it or not we are both left and right brained and, although you may function more strongly in one sphere, avoid the other at your peril if you want this new lifestyle of yours to work. Remember, you may be right brained, but at least half of your clients/galleries will be left brained. Creating a business plan and goal setting will help you to exercise your left-brain thinking and get the foundations in place on which you can build your career as an artist.

Creating a business plan

> *If you fail to plan, you plan to fail.*
> ~ Common saying, original author unknown

'A business plan for an artist?' you might say, 'You must be bloody mad!' But a career in art involves buying and selling and the fact is that you're a person in the business of art. We talk about 'artwork' – your artwork is a product, the same as an architect creates a building or a manufacturer makes a car.

Artists tend not to enjoy committing ideas to writing – which is the very reason that you will benefit from this plan. (It may also help convince the sceptics around you of the viability of your art career.) Like any businessperson, having a business plan can be a huge help in focusing your thinking.

I was asked at one point if I would accept a nomination for the Council of Business Women's 'Businesswoman of the Year' award. I eventually turned the nomination down because it involved attending three days of meetings (which I abhor) and I didn't feel it would really help my art business in terms of sales versus expenditure (I found out that you had to pay for your own flights, accommodation and so on.). Since initially, before the expenses dawned on me, I was enthusiastic, I spent a couple of days drawing up a business plan.

I derived a huge amount of value from the effort, albeit in hindsight! For the first time, I really acknowledged what I had achieved, but more importantly, I was able to think strategically about what I wanted in the future. As the Oracle of Delphi says, 'Man, know thyself'. As boring as it may appear, this exercise will help you to know yourself as you shift illusions about yourself, ground yourself and focus your thoughts.

Here is an idea for the outline of your art business plan:

1. Summary

A history of where you come from and why you've chosen art as a career.

2. Description of business

- *Motivation* – Why do you want to be an artist? This could be along the lines of: to live an inspired life and, in so doing, encourage others to do the same. (Or, it could be as simple as: to communicate the realities of life through the symbol of a sheep.)

- *Challenge* – Obstacles that you will need to overcome to create a viable business. One of the essential challenges is to continually explore with new ideas and styles in order to sustain interest in your work.

- *Service* – What services are you going to offer your purchasers? A unique product? The opportunity to connect with hidden aspects of their subconscious? Always delivering commissions timeously? Rebellious, challenging work? Or work done to the best of your ability (i.e. you are not afraid to reject work that you aren't 100% happy with)?

- *Variability* – How are you going to appeal to as broad a market as possible?

3. Market analysis

   - *Industry description and outlook* – What you have learnt about the art market locally or abroad.

   - *Target market* – Who do you see wanting to buy your art: the general public, private collectors, corporations? Try to define this even further: if you have a message, who do you most want to listen to that message?

   - *Competition* – You may feel you're in a league of your own, but realistically if you want to position yourself as a landscape artist, you'll have to examine just how many landscape artists there are (and some of them are really good). In your genre, look at whose work you most admire. What makes them stand out for you?

4. Marketing and sales strategy

   - *How do you plan to sell your work?* Through galleries, at private exhibitions, on the internet, or will you create your own gallery?

   - *How do you plan to make your market aware of your work?* A website devoted to your art is cool but how will you create traffic that results in sales?

5. How are you going to run your art business?

   - *Painting tracking* – How will you monitor which paintings are where?

   - *Administration* – Who will invoice and do the bookkeeping? How will this work?

   - *Website* – How will you keep your website updated and how often will you post new work?

- *Gallery visits* – Who will do this (will you employ an agent, persuade your partner to do it for you or visit the galleries yourself)? And how often will they/you go?

- *Wrapping and shipping* – Whose responsibility will this be?

- *Ordering materials* – Will you have back-up stock or will you order when you need it (and will this be practical in terms of timing)?

6. Management and ownership skills

- *Past experience* – What is it that has encouraged you to make it as an artist?

- *Special skills* – What unique abilities and talents do you possess to will assist you?

7. Suppliers

What materials do you see yourself using and do you have reliable delivery of these?

8. Funds required

How much capital are you going to need to sustain you in the start-up phase?

9. Future projects

Where do you see yourself heading?

10. Cashflow and budget (not strictly part of a business plan, but a useful addition nonetheless)

Write down month by month what you expect your income and expenses to be. If you know that you need £6000 a month to live, and if you realistically plan to create and sell five artworks a month valued at £1000 each, then you'll realize that there'll be a £1000 shortfall. How are you going to deal with that?

This type of specific information is hard to work with. Realism and artists tend not to go hand in hand (unless you're into Superrealism!). I know I would have gone kicking and screaming if I had had to do this exercise in the beginning. But ultimately it is true that the more specific you are about what you want to achieve, the greater your chance of success. Which is where goal setting comes in.

Does art make money?

Most artists will reply with a big 'NO!' The general public would prophesy gloom and poverty-filled doom. Yet there are artists who do make comfortable livings from their work. World-renowned British artist Damien Hirst even manages to employ a host of other artists to produce his ideas. (Hirst sees the real creative act as being the conception, not the execution, and that, as the progenitor of the idea, he is therefore the artist.)

Hirst's work entitled *The Physical Impossibility of Death in the Mind of Someone Living* involved a 4.3-metre shark in formaldehyde and became the ionic work of British art in the 1990s. When the work sold in 2004, only Jasper Johns surpassed the price fetched for the work of a living artist. Hirst surpassed Johns in 2007 with the sale of *Lullaby Spring* for US $19.2 million and in 2008 with the sale of *For the Love of God* for US $100 million. Not bad for work that was constructed not by the artist, but by a team of employees! If these figures start to boggle the mind, take the auction he held at Sotheby's in September 2008, where in an unprecedented move he bypassed his galleries and sold his entire show via auction. Exceeding all predictions, the show earned a whopping US $198 million.[1]

With numbers like these, the accountant in you might start waking up! Yet Hirst stands on the top of the pinnacle, just as JK Rowling does in the book world. Below Hirst is a triangle of earning potential, with the majority of artists finding themselves in the lowest section.

According to research done by the National Arts Council in 2003 in the UK, the average gross weekly earnings (before rent, materials, etc are deducted) from the art of an artist (i.e. not including any sideline jobs) was £230 per week. Of the artists surveyed, the average gross annual earnings of 83% of artists was less than £24,000. Of those, a third earned between £5930 and £11,851 and only 8% earned less than £5930. On the upper end of the scale, only 6.5% of the total respondents earned in the region of £36,500–£60,000.[2] While the dole would allow artists to survive at the lower end of the scale, being an artist for most people is considerably harder if you want to live a relatively comfortable life, unless you take on sideline jobs to supplement your art.

So, if your aspirations are to drive the latest 4×4, live on a country estate in Surrey and travel extensively in five-star luxury, then maybe you should accept that job as a stock broker. However, if it's quality of life you're after, then the life of an artist can be great. I may not live a life of luxury, but I had a wonderful beach walk this morning with a friend and our dogs, followed by a cappuccino watching the waves, before starting to paint at the studio with Anthony in the room next door. Later on my daughter, Anthony and I sat down to a salad lunch and a chat. My share portfolio is the time I share with friends and family – that's worth a lot of money to me!

That being said, it's no good taking long beach walks if you spend the time worrying about how you are going to pay the bills. So if you're going to be a full-time artist and you don't happen to have inherited a couple of million, then you're going to need to know how to make your career viable.

Catching a wake-up call?

When Anthony and I were still in our early 20s, we decided that designing T-shirts was a particularly chilled way to earn a living. The only way we could bring those designs into the market was to start our own business.

It was great – we were designing really hot surf heritage graphics. However, we had naïvely imagined that 95% of our time would involve design and 5% would involve selling into stores, organizing the manufacturing, screen-printing (which we did ourselves to save cost) and general admin. WRONG. The reverse was true. Suddenly we became bogged down with size graphs, invoicing, chasing up payments and pleading with stores to carry our range, with only 5% of the time doing what we actually loved.

Art, like anything else, requires administration, and admin is essential to your success. Unless you happen to have a partner who'll do it for you (and there are some artists who are lucky enough to have this!), you'll have to apply yourself to it, as much as you may view it as a drag.

The survey on British artists mentioned earlier found that artists spend on average less than half their time actually making their art. Annually, the time spent creating (using right-brain function) was only 45% of total activity time; nearly 10% was spent doing administration; 18% was spent working in another occupation; nearly 14% was spent on related art activities (workshops, teaching, etc); holidays accounted for just under 6%; studying less than 2%; and less than 1% was put down to unemployment, doing nothing or waiting between contracts and the remainder general activities.

So, being a viable artist does require being fairly busy – it's not going to work if you have fantasies about opting out of doing much and philosophizing rather than working. Like anything else, if you want to succeed you're going to have to work at it (and that includes left-brained admin!). Sorry.

Goal setting – Go ALL the way

Some things to consider:

- If you don't know where you're going, you'll end up nowhere.

- Goals give you short-term motivation and long-term vision.

- The clearer your goals, the better chance you have of succeeding.

- Writing your goals down and monitoring them weekly gives you a higher chance of success.

- The more you succeed in achieving your goals, the more you build self-confidence which allows you more chance of succeeding on the next stage of your journey.

The following is an exercise you can do for all aspects of your life or simply for your goals as an artist.

Exercise
Write down the 'big picture' of what you want from your life as an artist in five years' time. Be creative and give as much detail as possible (saying, 'Being an artist' is not enough).

Are there specific artistic goals you want to achieve?

Maybe it's a certain gallery you want to be in, somewhere overseas you'd like to visit, or an artistic town you want to live in. Do you have a family? If so, how do you see them fitting in to your picture?

How does your partner fit into your plan?

How much do you want to be earning (take inflation into account)?

What will you do in your free time?

Is there a way that you would like to give back to the world? Maybe you'd like to teach, motivate others or encourage art development in underprivileged communities?

Why do you want to achieve these goals? Be honest with yourself. Is it to please or impress a partner? Maybe one of your parents wanted to be an artist and you are fulfilling their dream – but is it yours? Do you want to opt out of society? To find yourself? To become famous? To make your corporate friends envious of your laidback lifestyle? Is it because art is your passion? Because you're tired of your lousy boss? Because it's a cool thing to do? Or because you feel you haven't succeeded at anything else? Keep asking yourself until all the answers emerge – it's a bit like peeling the layers of an onion until you get to the underlying reason for your desire to be an artist. Remember that no reason is wrong.

Now look at what could be holding you back from being successful. List belief systems that may subconsciously be sabotaging you (we covered this in Chapter 1).

Break down your goal into annual stages. Now look at the year ahead, and break it down into monthly goals, all focused on the end goal. Look at the following month and decide what you want to achieve by then. Then break the goal down into weekly – and then daily – stages. Finally, create a day-to-day list of things you need to be doing if your long-term goal is to be met. Once again, be as specific as possible.

Make a discipline of spending a couple of minutes each day reviewing what you have achieved, and keep the process going by creating goals for the following days. From time to time, review your long-term plans, which may need to be adjusted according to your shifting needs and what you have learnt since setting them.

Keeping the following tips in mind will help you:

- **Be positive**: 'Explore five different styles, and find one that really works for me' is a far more encouraging goal than 'Don't mess up'.

- **Set priorities**: What inspires you most will be the focus of your greatest effort. The opposite is obviously also true, but remember that some attention to your least inspiring tasks may be crucial to your success. Bad bookkeeping will lose paintings and the money you are wanting to earn. It's not fun, but is essential. List in order the things that are most important for you to achieve, for example, 'Develop a recognizable style' would take preference over 'Finish five paintings'. This will help focus you.

- **Detail**: The more specific you are, the greater your chances of success. Give dates, financial amounts, times, and go into detail about what you want to achieve and by when. Our egos loathe this type of exercise – if you are resisting this, that's the ego talking!

- **Make the goals obtainable**: Writing down that you want to earn £50,000 in the first month may not be realistic. A good measure is to set goals that are 20% out of your comfort zone. It's better to set smaller daily goals and achieve them than to set a huge annual goal that cannot realistically be met. As you achieve each daily goal, you'll build confidence in your abilities for the day ahead.

- **Base goals on issues within your control**: Having a goal such as 'Approach two galleries with my portfolio' is within your control. 'Have two galleries accept my work' is out of your control and can be dispiriting if you don't achieve that goal, through no fault of your own.

- **Reward yourself**: For each goal that you achieve along the way, take time out to appreciate what you've done and do something that inspires you.

- **Review your achievement**: If you feel you've met a goal too easily, then you may need to up your game plan. If, in hindsight, a goal has been too difficult, then ease up a little the following week. Also review how what you've learnt affects your long-term plan. With the insight you've gained, change things along the way if it feels right.

- **Inspiration**: Remember that we need to feel inspired by our end goal. If you feel manipulated into choosing a certain goal, chances are you will resist achieving it. Make sure your goal is just that – yours!

What's the point of this?

- Focusing on what's important to you gives you a place to aim towards, rather than wandering around aimlessly.

- It also lets you focus on what really has meaning for you.

- As an artist you can't rely on others to motivate you. This process allows you to motivate yourself.

- We are not born with self-confidence – we develop it with our achievements.

No set task = no sense of achievement = no self-confidence. Self-confidence (rather than ego-based arrogance) will help you hugely in your goal of being an artist.

Why articulating your goals is a seriously powerful tool

Visualize the two dimensions of your mind: the conscious and the subconscious. The conscious is like a super-nerd (skinny, glasses, weak but oh-so-bright), while the subconscious is more like a seriously thick army robot. This robot is super-strength powerful – makes the Incredible Hulk look like a ballet dancer. It doesn't question, but only acts on orders given, which it takes literally. It also doesn't operate in the past or the future, but only in the present. Everything is now.

Say you have a goal like this: 'I want to be a successful artist selling abundantly'. The conscious nerdy character gets excited: 'Yay, yippee, yay! This will be fun!' The subconscious awaits instructions.

When the subconscious gets the order from the conscious it acts accordingly, no questions asked. 'I want to . . .' translates into 'I will *want* to be an artist' (but not necessarily *be* an artist). That is why saying, 'I am a successful artist' is much more powerful – the subconscious reads that as an instruction which it simply needs to make happen.

So, while the conscious may have the ability to conceive the plan, it has no power to implement it, whereas the subconscious is responsible for achieving what you want. If your subconscious and conscious are working together then anything is truly possible.

We might have become a bit slack when it comes to our subconscious. If you have frequently said you will do something – be it going to the gym, calling a client or writing a letter – and you have not done it by the time you said you would, then your subconscious has habitually learnt that what you say = not what you do. Being non-questioning, now that you are telling it to make you a success and get your art out there, it reverts to what it has been taught. To reprogramme the confused subconscious you have to start doing what you say you will, by when you say you will. Now your word is true to itself.

Simple, I know, yet we find it so hard to be true to our word. Life coaches estimate that we only do what we say we will by when we say we will 15–25% of the time. And that's when we've actually committed to doing something in the first place.

This simple tool of being true to your word, when applied religiously, will have a quantum affect on your life and your ability to achieve your dreams.

Notes

1. Taken from http://en.wikipedia.org/wiki/Damien_Hirst, accessed 16 October 2010.
2. Taken from New Earnings Survey Office for National Statistics (Nomis), *Crown Copyright*, published in Davies and Lindley, 2003, on Arts Council England's website (http://www.artscouncil.org.uk), accessed 30 August 2009.

5

How can I be marketable?

The three things I look for in an artist are:
Creative, unique and marketable artwork.
Quality and presentation of work.
Passion.

~ Margaret Campbell-Ryder, The Red Hill Gallery

Artistic vs creative

It is a common belief that artistic means the same thing as creative. Through a lifetime of working with artistic and creative people, I have noticed that there is a big distinction between the two.

An artist may be technically proficient in his or her chosen media and can create aesthetically pleasing works. A creative person may lack some technical proficiency but have superior skills when it comes to thinking out of the box or creating fresh approaches or concepts. Artistic people may be able to create exquisite renditions but can't think up fresh ideas, whereas creative people may have thousands of ideas, but lack the artistic skills to implement them. Nevertheless, a creative person may conceptualize art in new and different ways.

Sometimes, as in the case of Leonardo da Vinci, the artistic and creative skills meet. While there are few artists who aren't at least a bit creative and vice versa, most of us tend to be more one or the other. But being a creative person in a formal art class painting realistic still lives could be a somewhat frustrating experience. Similarly, an artistic person who feels pressure to be 'different' could find this stressful.

Knowing which aspect you lean towards will help you decide what type of art you'll be happiest and most successful producing.

Creative people are good at:	Artistic people are good at:
Concepts	Aesthetics
Thinking	Feeling
Original ideas	Technical skills
Quirky drawing	Realistic drawing

When I had to write reviews for an online website, I was amazed at how the same subjects came up time and time again in many artists' works. More often than not they were painted in the same style, often using the same compositions for the same subject matter, to greater or lesser degrees of competency. Had these artists realized that they fell more into the artistic side of things, they could have sought the assistance of a more creative person to encourage conceptual skills – and given their work more buyer appeal.

People have been painting landscapes for centuries. What differentiates one artist from another is the ability to create a unique style. To do this, we sometimes have to step away from the technical and enter the realms of the creative. Likewise, if you identify yourself as being highly creative, then taking a few art lessons to learn techniques may make you a far better artist.

Exercise

As an exercise, review your own personal art history. Would you say your strength lies more in the idea or the rendition?

Tapping your unique talent

> *Easily one's doing can become an undoing.*
> *Art either does – or does not – take on a life apart from its maker.*
>
> ~ Michael Stevenson, Michael Stevenson Gallery

A woman had the desire to be an artist. Enthusiasm gushed from every pore. She was motivated and prepared to leave the day job – and she wanted my feedback. Problem was, as I sat looking at the art she had spread around me, I felt she had no natural artistic ability. You might say that art is in the eye of the beholder (and I'd agree) but in this case it was obvious that there was no sense of colour, no feel for composition, no design sense and no conceptual thinking. Her painting simply consisted of badly painted shapes in colours that did not work.

It was a difficult position to be in and one that had me wishing I was anywhere but there at that moment. How do you tell someone not to give up their day job? I instantly felt sympathy for galleries whose job it is to break that news to aspiring artists on a daily basis.

It had happened before that someone believing there was a quick buck to be made from art had showed me the work she planned to take to a large gallery. Not in a million years would the gallery have accepted the work (and subsequently didn't) – however, in that instance, I had lacked the courage to say so.

It's not to say that neither of these people could have become successful artists in time, but neither had been painting for longer than a month. (That's a bit like going to the gym for the first time and putting your name down for the Iron Man finals.) Art, like anything else, takes work – and while the length of time you've been painting does not denote quality as such, sometimes people's belief in their abilities is exaggerated, blinding them to reality. This can cause much heartache along the way. Just as the Chinese believe that a mandolin player is created over a number of lifetimes, the same could be said of a great artist. So, if your mum thinks your creations are great, that's not necessarily a clear indication of its quality.

Try to glean honest feedback from as many people knowledgeable about art as possible. Their feedback will be invaluable. Study artists; learn to understand individual artists' work. Go to galleries, read magazines, familiarize yourself with different artistic genres. Explore, learn, discover, absorb and above all be absolutely honest with yourself in terms of your strengths and weaknesses. Be open to input and learning.

Remember as well that Piet Mondrian was an extremely talented artist, yet his very definitive style meant that being able to draw human figures in detail was not essential to his art. William Turner's ability to capture the mood in a landscape is superb – however, being highly conceptual was not essential to his chosen style. Examine your weaknesses, acknowledge them and work with your strengths. A poorly drawn figure is not going to do your reputation any good, but your superb colour choice might.

Finding your own style

> I look for good technique and something different that stands out from the rest of what is out there.
> ~ Lisa King, Lisa King Gallery

Think of the great artists. Didn't they find unchartered waters and navigate them, even when they were ridiculed for their efforts? Frida Kahlo's unconventional work was mostly dismissed during her lifetime while her husband (who has now joined the ranks of relatively obscure artists) claimed the honours. Van Gogh's work, as well as the other impressionists, was considered outrageous at the time and not worthy of exhibition. Picasso, Warhol, Miro, Lichtenstein, Pollock and many others broke boundaries and established inroads by doing what pleased them.

It is a thin line between pleasing yourself and pleasing your market – especially if you enter the world of galleries selling art for people's homes. But if the truth be told, I have spent years doing weird and wondrous work to please myself which did not sell (who would want a room full of plaster hands or DIY blocks to construct your own 3D art entitled 'Art, you figure it out'?). I have to say that allowing myself a degree of commercialism and having people call me with orders is a lot more fun than wondering how to get rid of 90 rubber knives or 50 plaster hands! (Even though I enjoyed creating them and still do conceptual art from time to time.)

Having blinkers is bonkers – why research is essential

When considering a new artist we look for work that is of quality and which the artist clearly takes pride in. We look for work that is commercially viable and would appeal to our audience and would hang well with work we already display. We need to know that the artist is not already exhibiting their work in other local galleries so that we are offering our audience something new and eye-catching.

~ Laura Cole, Art at Five Gallery

To aspiring artists who mean to make a living from their craft, there is really only one important piece of advice I can give and that is MARKETING. Art is business. The first question an artist should ask themselves is 'Who is going to buy this work?'

~ Di Smith, G2 Art Gallery

I was in a successful gallery and was saying how much I liked a particular artist's work. The curator agreed, saying however that she did not like the artist's new direction. She added that when she had told the artist her feelings, he had not responded kindly to her feedback.

While one can't alter one's style every time somebody criticizes it, you have to be aware that the curators and those who work in galleries are privy to comments and feedback from the public that you are not. They also know what sells in their galleries. So ignoring their input may be unwise if you want to sell your work.

I met a man who had just sold his company and now wanted to paint full time. I am always hesitant when asked to give feedback on another artist's work because:

a) I might just not like the work, which doesn't mean it's not good.
b) If the work is simply bad, I never know if I should say so in order to spare them further humiliation from the galleries. It's my experience tactfully saying things like, 'You need to develop this further . . .' usually gets ignored.
c) Who can really judge another's work?

Initially I managed to dodge the issue by making small talk, but I couldn't avoid the art, which was hanging all over the walls. It was amateurish, boring, lacking in technical skill and the subject matter was so overdone that it held little appeal. When probed, I attempted (probably rather badly) to subtly suggest that he look at various art galleries and see how his work compared. I also suggested that if he wanted to create a stir (as opposed to a yawn), he try looking at new ways of approaching either the subject matter or the style.

The hint was not taken. Instead he spoke about not wanting to 'prostitute' himself, or get some gallery owner to assess his work and that frankly they could 'take it or leave it'. (It was pretty clear the latter would be the case.) While I understood that his arrogance masked his fear, I also knew that unless he was able to overcome his fear, his chances of developing his work were not good (and the chances of making a living from his art severely jeopardized).

The moral of the story is: be open to other artists' work, see what they are doing right and learn from it, so you can improve your game plan. Never be afraid to reinvent yourself – the more times you do it, the less scary it becomes. I recall just after selling a painting I'd won the (SASA) South African Art Society's 'Best Acrylic' with, I desperately wanted to buy it back. On some level I feared that I would never reach that standard again – it would be my one-hit wonder. I confess (rather embarrassingly) that I tried to make a close resemblance of the work, but it never did have the same vibe and I ended up destroying the second work. It was a great lesson though, because it forced me to move on.

Research is very important. Take an avid interest in art. Be aware of both the local and international art market. Shows and exhibitions are a great way of gauging the response to your work – every time I do a show I come back with enormous insight into what works and what does not. I listen to the comments because many times people do not realize that I'm the artist. Positive or negative, it's all good in helping me understand my work. One of the more amusing incidences was listening to a teacher explain some of my earlier work to her pupils. It was fascinating – not at all what I had actually been thinking/feeling when doing it! She was seeing her own interpretation – which was great and gave me new ideas to explore.

In one of my sideline jobs while attempting to get financially free enough to focus on art and writing, I took on the task of writing 25 art critiques a month for an art website. After waxing lyrical on 25 artists each month, I must have used up every adjective that ever was and a few I invented for the occasion! My husband questioned what he saw as my folly, but I am so grateful for the experience. To find 25 artists out of the several thousand whose work I enjoyed or could at least appreciate, I had to wade through numerous artists' web pages, and it gave me a wonderful overview of art. I learnt so much that it was well worth the effort.

Your childhood angst won't match the lounge curtains

If you choose to sell through more commercial galleries who specialize in work for offices and private homes, be careful that the subjects you choose are appropriate.

At an exhibition in Europe I started chatting to a woman I'd gravitated towards as we both spoke English. She told me that her husband had given up his comfortable 9–5 job in the UK and relocated to Tenerife (where the cost of living was considerably less) in order for him to fulfil his lifetime dream of being an artist. The years and savings were ticking by without her husband being able to earn any income from his art. To date, kindly relatives and friends had been the sole purchasers. She was obviously worried about the situation and his seeming indifference towards the problem. After chatting to her for some time, I was curious to see her husband's painting to understand why he wasn't having much luck selling.

The answer was obvious when I saw the work. It was full of tortured-looking souls and writhing, bloodied bodies. Any amateur psychologist could have seen that the angst he wasn't showing her was being painted into his art. In short, while technically proficient, the works would not be what you'd hang in your lounge; neither were they conceptually interesting enough to hang in a more avant-garde gallery. The artist lived in a tourist haven and so it stood to reason that they would be his biggest potential customers. Would the average Brit on holiday want to remember the experience with the image of a flayed body?

If the artist wanted to make a viable income from his work, then he would have take into account his market and possibly rethink his subject matter. As an artist wanting to earn a living from art, one cannot disregard the needs of the client any more than a cereal manufacturer can, or the makers of soap.

This is where many artists struggle. Having spent a lifetime submitting to the needs of bosses, clients and colleagues, art often represents the freedom of 'doing what I want to do'. The realization that a certain amount of 'prostitution' may be necessary is uncomfortable. Yet artists who are earning a good living inevitably produce work which adheres (to a certain degree) to the demands of the public. A good way around this is to have a commercial portfolio which gives you financial freedom, and then also devoting a certain amount of time to exploring other styles and areas of your art (which may, in turn, develop into art that does sell).

There are, of course, extremes and into this category I would place 'pet portraits' or portraits of people who don't particularly interest you but which you do simply for a commission. Yet even if you have to paint pet portraits (under a pseudonym, preferably) while you build your career, in my opinion that's more fun than being a waitress.

'Hey,' I can hear you say, 'I'll paint what and how I want and I'm not prepared to be that commercial'. That's OK, but either you will have to find a gallery that supports your work, or realize that your old corporate job may well come back into your life. Or you may have to supplement your income by giving classes or working part-time until your work is appreciated.

Painting across more than one style

> *Never balk at the idea of having a commercial line. Sometimes to enable you to progress and stay creative, you need to put food on the table. Having said that, never compromise yourself or your talent for that commercial line.*
> ~ Di Smith, G2 Gallery

Many artists, either for a business or creative reason, choose to paint across more than one signature style. This certainly makes sense in that each style enables a different artist persona; different styles can fulfil different galleries' and consumers' needs and increase your chances of selling. It also makes you less vulnerable to fluctuating markets.

There is the view, though, that if you paint across too many styles, you lose your identity altogether (like those knock-off paintings from the East that sell for next to nothing, where the artist is completely incidental). If you choose this multi-style route, then try at least to keep some common stylistic links. For instance, if colour is your strong point, let it weave its way through your landscapes, abstracts and nudes.

Why copying doesn't work long term

Copied work is not what curators are looking for.

'Yes, I know your work! In fact, a friend of mine saw it in a gallery. She liked it so much she took photos with her cell phone and then copied it for her husband's office.' That's an (almost) direct quote, and I was the artist they were referring to!

Often when I work at shows people don't seem to realize that I am the artist, and they will comment on the work as if I am invisible. How about this one (these were two eyeing my work at a show):

'What do you think of this?'

'My five-year-old could do it.'

'Yes, but I like it. That's why I'm copying some of them for my lounge.'

I actually received a phone call the other day from a young artist saying she had copied some of my work for her boyfriend's office. His boss had liked it so much they wanted to commission her to do paintings in the same style (mine – I have a very distinctive style) for the whole office and would I mind as she could do with the money! I had to thank her for having the integrity to call me, but was amazed that the perception was that I'd be happy with this arrangement.

Amateurs copying an established artist's work is irritating, but it's less offensive than when a so-called professional artist copies the work of another artist. It's very tempting when one comes across a successful artist's work to emulate it – it appears to offer a blueprint for your own success. However, this seldom works long term. Not only do you run the very real risk of being sued by the artist, but who wants to be known as the artist who copies? Copied work will always be second best, as the spectre of the other artist looms over your shoulder. Rather persevere and find your own path.

Now, there's no harm at all in learning from other artists by emulating their styles. Sting once said that he learns to play other musicians' songs in order to understand their music. So use other work as a stepping stone. Finding your own style is like finding yourself and liking what you see!

A young artist, tired of being turned down by numerous galleries, opened his own shop in a new shopping mall, with the intention of painting and selling his work in the premises. In order to attract clientele he painted abstracts, which were currently popular 'decorator's dream' art, similar to a number of other successful artists. In the beginning business boomed as the undiscerning public bought these recognizable pieces at a fraction of the cost of the original artists' works. However, six months later he was forced to close his gallery as interest and sales dwindled.

What went wrong? There is obviously no definitive answer, but I believe he made two mistakes:

1) He only stocked his own work in the gallery and so only covered a small sector of the potential art-buying market. Having other artists' work would have thrown the net wider.

2) Because he did not have his own style, he drew his style from other artists' work. And many other artists, seeing a style that was easy to copy (which had originated from two well-respected artists), jumped onto the band wagon and flooded the market with similar works, which went out of fashion as quickly as the curtains and matching sofas would. The two established artists had already moved on and continued their careers successfully, while those that had emulated their styles were unable to reinvent themselves.

One gallery owner I deal with and who has 17 years' experience in the business was horrified to find that one of her top artist's work bore a less-than-comfortable resemblance to an artist in another country. A client had purchased one of the local artist's works and then emigrated and discovered the original artist's work. He immediately saw the resemblance and, being justifiable angry, had notified the local gallery owner. Worried about how much more of his work was 'inspired' by other artists, the gallery owner was reluctant to continue stocking his work. Trust – the foundation stone of a good relationship – had been broken.

Galleries often select artists that complement each other but that are not too similar – there would be no point. Most reputable gallery owners would never dream of stocking work that closely resembled an established artist's work – it would jeopardize their reputation and the ongoing good relationships they already have with their artists. Of course, you do get exceptions – those galleries who have been known to persuade enthusiastic young artists to copy work and then sell it to them for a fraction of the cost. The less said about these the better!

I have experienced a 'copycat' who attempted to reproduce the style and nature of my work. Fortunately, all the galleries who stock my work stood firmly behind me. The work itself was a poor imitation, but it did cause confusion in the marketplace. This practice is more commonplace than one would expect and is, sadly and ironically, part of an industry in which creativity and innovation should flourish.

Know your market

Anthony loves painting nudes and has been successful doing so. However, he learnt a valuable lesson in the beginning. He did some fairly erotic nudes but soon learnt that not everyone is as comfortable with the human body as he is. While people may admire a nude in a gallery, when it comes to hanging it in their home a degree of conservatism comes into play. Full-frontal nudes don't sell as well as tastefully draped ones, and nine times out of ten customers will opt for more discreet poses. Even if buyers are comfortable with nudes, they may feel they are not suitable for other family members, like children. There are some galleries who, on principle, won't stock nudes.

It's worth getting a sense of who you are dealing with – both in terms of your final customers and the galleries you sell to. I heard of a gallery owner who turned down a whole batch of paintings when he heard that the artist took drugs. And from my own experience: I sold a large work entitled *George's Bush,* only to have it returned when the client ran into some flack from his pro-Bush buddies.

So, do you please yourself and paint what you like? Tricky one. Personally, I step over the edge sometimes, if I have an idea that appeals to me, or a statement that I feel needs to be made, but I am very careful about choosing the gallery I put the work into.

Other forms of art

Much has been written in the art world about the demise of painting. And it is true that art has taken so many different forms – kinetic art, installation art, graffiti art, interactive art, video art, performance art, fractal art, conceptual art, environmental art, digital art, art happenings, etc – that painting might be viewed as the fancy of blue-rinsed ladies *en plein air* on a Sunday afternoon.

However, there are a huge amount of homeowners and corporations wanting something to put on the walls, where more edgy art won't work. To the *cognoscenti* of the art world, galleries that sell work to the man in the street are often treated with distain. So-called 'mall' galleries are seen as commercial and not really hanging 'true' art.

Yet in the UK's *Modern Painters* or the USA's *Art Now*, the majority of the featured work is done on a canvas, even if it is not viewed as cutting edge. Art that hangs on walls is still the most popular visual art form, because it has the most potential clients. (Personally, I like to play with different forms of art on my free day.)

Titles

Damien Hirst mentioned in an interview that he spends a huge amount of time thinking up titles for his work. *Nude (12)* or *Abstract (9)* just don't have the same magic as *Young Girl Eating Mangoes* or *Song of Eternal Life Consequences*. Long after I've forgotten the actual work, titles such as Joseph Beuys's *I Like America and America Likes Me* stay in my memory and continue to amuse.

A title will also help the viewer to access what was in your mind when creating the work (particularly if the work is more abstract). Avoid clichés unless they are integral to the concept (like when you are being ironic). Captivating, romantic, outrageous, shocking, intriguing or just plain over the top, titles can sell paintings and are worth spending the time to conceive.

While there are many who would not agree, and would prefer the obvious *Landscape Sketch, January 2009* or *Still Life 2009*, if you're an artist, be creative!

Some titles I love:

- *A Lifetime of Enthusiasm* – William Kentridge

- *What Would Neil Young Do?* – Jeremy Deller

- *Star Bright, Star Might* – Kate Gilmore

- *The Bride Stripped Bare by Her Bachelors* – Marcel Duchamp

- *The Sun Is Not Ridiculous* – Schandra Singh

- *Hue Never Know* – Lisa Kereszi

Numbering your work

After completing every painting, as a matter of course, I photograph it and number it according to the year it was produced. This way, if someone contacts me about a painting, I know exactly which one they are referring to. Surprisingly, even some of the larger, more established galleries don't have their own codes. Without some form of reference other than the title, particularly if titles are similar or duplicate (*Seaside 1* and *Seaside 2*, for instance, are very easy to confuse), you can get into a big muddle over what work is where.

If your coding system is efficient it will reduce your stress levels in the long run. Having the year the work was done is also an essential part of the process. With digital cameras the process can be speedily executed. And should you one day become famous, at least you'll have a record of all your works in easily printable form!

6

Engaging with galleries

A critical component of us deciding to work with a new artist or photographer is if they will shift our perceptions. If they do not imperceptibly alter the way we look at an aspect of the world, even though the images may be very accomplished in a formal sense, we could not show the work in the context of contemporary art practice. It is the critical engagement with the visual traditions and the integrity of the conceptual intent that is our first concern.

~ Michael Stevenson, Michael Stevenson Gallery

Different types of galleries want different types of work

To open a gallery, all you need is a venue (luckily, shabby chic is in), some means of hanging, a few lights, a sign and the knowledge that you'll shortly be inundated with hopeful artists wanting to cover your walls with their work, which you won't have to pay for until it's actually sold. It seems a dead cert. Besides which, you don't actually need to know anything about art itself. (I have experienced serious cringe-worthy moments with gallery owners who go blank when you mention the likes of Sam Taylor-Wood, David Hockney, Tracey Emin or even Matisse or Miro.)

While the more successful gallery owners are extremely knowledgeable, sadly this is not always the case. So many people open galleries and many fall by the wayside, sometimes dragging a few artists with them.

In approaching galleries, there are two basic types to keep in mind: those that aim their work at the man in the street, corporations, and so on, and those who sell more to collectors and can consequently showcase performance, video, installation and conceptual art. While the former type of gallery tends to exhibit mainly the work of local artists, the latter often exhibits work from artists around the globe. Obviously this is a broad generalization, but it bears thinking about when it comes to deciding just what sort of an artist you are or want to be. If doing attractive abstract or realistic landscapes of the surrounding area is your interest, then you will be aiming at the former type of gallery. If you have created an entire boat made of feathers and a shoal of lead fish (a really great piece at Florence Biennale 2007 – artist unknown), the latter type of gallery may be interested in your work.

What are the pros and cons of each?

Most 'general' galleries keep portfolios of artists who cut across the spectrum of their clients' needs. So you may find an abstract artist, a realistic landscape painter or two, something more edgy, something more expressionistic and so on. As an art 'supplier', you will be viewed from the perspective of what gap you can potentially fill. If your work is very similar to an established artist they already promote, they may not be keen to hang your work – even if it's really good. These galleries are usually very familiar with their market, and they have a good idea of what's saleable or not. In other words, the decision of whether or not to hang your work will be a commercial rather than a personal decision.

A disadvantage of working with galleries designed to sell to the general public is that if you become known for a certain style of work and if there is a demand for that style, you may find yourself caught between wanting to move in a different direction and the very obvious commercial benefits of producing more of the same. As one artist put it, after churning out numerous – but successful – flowers in the same loose style, 'It's become an exercise in experimenting with different colours'.

If you choose to target the second type of gallery, you will be freer to do what you choose, with little public interference. However, because much of what you produce may be either too edgy or too impractical to install in the average home or office, you will have to capture and maintain the attention not only of like-minded galleries, but also of collectors who are prepared to buy, for example, a head made of your frozen blood (Damien Hirst). And it goes without saying that there are far fewer of these types of purchasers.

What will a gallery do for me (apart from the obvious)?

> *An artist should expect a gallery to: market and promote their work, sell to the best of their ability and be loyal to the artist.*
> ~ Margaret Campbell-Ryder, The Red Hill Gallery

> *An artist can expect the gallery to represent them professionally and to the best of their ability. They should expect the gallery to be knowledgeable regarding details surrounding the work and the artist; work can then be confidently sold and any customer questions answered. The artist should also expect good communication from the gallery regarding feedback from visitors, as well as sales that are made.*
> ~ Laura Cole, The Art at Five Gallery

Once you've been taken on by a gallery, you'll find that they are (hopefully!) great at promoting your work through their websites, advertising, PR, exhibitions and so on. This not only gives your work credibility but also exposes you to a broader market. Galleries are often approached by people

71

looking for artists for various promotional events or commissions to which you would otherwise not have access. Larger galleries may also have contacts that can move your work into an international market.

Gallery staff need to know the background, achievements and so on of the artist they are selling. When one gallery told a relative that one of Anthony's works was actually one of mine and even argued the case, I had to seriously question our being in the gallery, where clearly staff were not knowledgeable about each artist.

In a good gallery, you'll have an interested party willing to act as a sounding board, to give advice and to chase down clients who are not keen to part with their cash. They will also fight for your rights should the need arise. So, even while you're on holiday relaxing on the beach, someone in a gallery somewhere is working to sell your art. It's oh so nice (as you sip that second Mai Tai cocktail) getting a call to say you've sold another work or have received a large commission. Yay for galleries!

How galleries make a living

Self-funded galleries

Some galleries are funded by their sales entirely and often have to charge high commissions to survive – up to 80–120% mark-up from the artist's price (this amount usually decreases as the price of the work increases). It's unusual for galleries to add 100% onto the artist's price (so if the artist lets the gallery have the painting for £3000, the gallery retails it for £6000 plus VAT). High rental costs, staff costs and the general running expenses mean that only galleries in smaller towns are able to survive with a lower mark-up.

Artist-run or funded galleries

These are galleries where local artists club together and run their own galleries, splitting costs and often taking turns working in the galleries. Staff overheads are usually much lower in these galleries, meaning lower mark-ups on the actual work or bigger margins for the artists. Some galleries may be fortunate enough to be funded or supported by government or company funding, which is beneficial for the artist who can earn more per piece.

'Vanity' or 'glamour' galleries

These are becoming more common and some galleries operate both as more conventional galleries and as 'vanity' galleries, either by segregating spaces or running a certain amount of exhibitions that are artist funded annually. The artists then buy space on the wall or in the gallery for a certain period of time, and so rely more on these 'rentals' than on actual sales to fund them. By charging artists to hang their work, they can't really lose since the artist is in effect buying space, any sales are simply an added bonus. Some of them do however take less commission as a result.

If they contact you, these types of galleries send flowery, flattering letters telling you how wonderful your art is and how much they would like to see it in their gallery. You feel 'found'. There may even have been a 'selection process', and you'll be feeling pretty chuffed with yourself until somewhere in the small print you find that there are rather large costs involved over and above simply shipping the work there.

I had a New York gallery contact me the other day and the cost to exhibit seemed fairly reasonable until I read about the 'Promotional' expenses, which consisted of:

1. **Exhibition catalogue**: Full production – graphic design and printing.
2. **Catalogue essay** written by a professional New York-based art critic.
3. **Advertising** in an art magazine at a discounted rate.
4. **Public relations** consisting of:
   - securing a minimum of one review about Artist's work in a New York art publication
   - compiling and distributing press-packages (press-release, invitation, and catalogue) among collectors, critics, and curators.

Admittedly these were optional and I could select all or some of the options depending on my budget, but I suspect that my 'selection' would not have been based as much on my work as the money I was prepared to throw at the event. Now it's not hard to imagine who might be running or profiteering from the printing, PR and so on.

All is not completely lost, though. If you have the capital, this process can get you an international gallery exhibition to add to your CV. If you accompany the work, you'll have the chance to interact and network with other artists (you are seldom the only artist on exhibit), you'll be exposed to a variety of different art, a holiday that is tax deductible (provided you are earning a living that reaches the taxable income mark), a chance to travel, exposure to a foreign audience and maybe (if you are extremely lucky) the opportunity to get into other galleries. However, there are no guarantees and some artists have returned dejected and considerably (financially) poorer from the experience. An Italian gallery approached me along these lines, but having spent a bit of time on the internet and spoken to other artists who had exhibited there, I decided that the cost vs benefits did not work for me.

Possible pitfalls include: if locals know that the standard of work at a particular gallery is dubious, they might give the gallery a wide berth; you often have no say as to how or where your work will be hung; certain artists may be given preference in position or space, leaving you to question whether they just paid more.

There is also the huge cost of getting your work to overseas venues and back. Courier companies work on a volumetric weight (length × depth × height ÷ 5000 = volumetric weight). For example, 150cm × 10cm × 200cm = 300,000 ÷ 5000 = 60kg. So although pieces of work may only weigh a couple of kilograms in *actual* weight, the volumetric weight is higher. In the example above, for the work that actually only weighs, say, 5kg, you'll be paying for 60kg. This is why rolling up a painting makes a lot of sense if you can do so.

'Find me good artists'

It may surprise you, but this is the plea of many galleries. The trouble is that they are looking for really good and innovative original work and most of what they see does not meet these criteria. Many artists are not benefiting from the enthusiasm of the galleries because they are recycling styles or subjects. For someone who combines good technical skills and interesting themes with a unique style, doors will open. If galleries are not accepting your work, blaming them is not going to help. Rather, review your work and look for ways to improve upon what you are doing.

Commitment

If you still have your day job, galleries may not see you as being serious about your work. Ideally they want to deal with artists who are committed enough to be full-time artists. If you are still making the transition, you'll have to demonstrate that you will be able to fulfil commissions even though you are still working in another job.

Choosing a gallery to approach

I often hear artists refer to galleries as if they were 'The Enemy', as if somehow they have all conspired together and decided to torment the artist by refusing to take their work. If you are caught in this trap and galleries are not taking you on board, then ask yourself:

- Is my work of a sufficiently high standard?

- Is the look and feel original?

- Is the technique good?

- Is my thinking original?

- Am I choosing the right gallery for my style of work?

- Who would buy my work? Are those people in this gallery?

Researching a gallery first can also spare you humiliation later. If it's an edgy, trendy gallery with avant-garde video installations, then taking in a portfolio of works entitled *Seaside Cottages (1–6)* or *Sunset at Lizard Point* is going to leave you feeling ridiculous. So will walking into a gallery adorned with paintings of flamboyant flowers and sad, wide-eyed portraits of children with your piece entitled *Sexual Imaginings of a Corporate Hermaphrodite, Series One.*

Once you have researched a suitable gallery, if at all possible, find out their work ethic by speaking to the artists they represent. I have had a gallery lose a number of paintings. I had been warned prior to displaying my work there that other artists had had problems with them, but chose to ignore the warning.

Certain galleries may not want you to approach them directly, rather choosing to select artists themselves. Michael Stevenson from the Michael Stevenson Gallery says:

> *Galleries like to discover artists – that is part of the initial courtship. Thus, thrusting your work in the face of a gallery is a kiss of death. Exhibit it and present it where opportunities present themselves, and let galleries come across it in those contexts. If it has merit, they will come across it because it is in galleries' interests to discover the best of the bright young things.*

Once again, doing your homework will give you the information you need for different galleries.

Sending proposals to galleries

The traditional way of approaching galleries is to send a proposal showing the type of work you do, enclosing a brief CV and an artist's statement and, naturally, a covering letter.

- **Covering letter**: This should briefly introduce who you are and give the reason for your letter. (Using the addressee's name is far better than a generic 'Dear gallery owner'.) This can be followed by any noteworthy achievements, an artist's statement (this can also be a separate document), a few words as to why your work would suit their gallery and a conclusion giving your contact details and website. Make sure the letter is correctly worded and spelt – remember, you want to look professional. You can email the whole package, but I have noticed a higher rate of response from sending hard copies than easy-to-delete emails.

- **CV**: Keep this specific to your art career. Knowing you were in sales for eight years and lengthy details about your schooling, unless it's relevant to the form your art has taken, is of little relevance to a busy gallery owner. It may help listing other galleries who have your work.

- **Artist's statement**: Just because you understand that your work embodies an 'endless sequence of substitutes and missed encounters' and shows an interest in 'the corporeal and the sensuous, but also in the unforeseeable and the unstable',[1] does not mean that the viewer or the gallery owner will. It has been said that good art does not require a lengthy justification, but you do need to convey your aims, relevant themes, materials used (particularly if unconventional) and any influences that may have affected you.

- **Visual portfolio**: In the past, artists relied on slide presentations or photographs. Today you can upload any number of works onto a CD, which is cost effective and easy to view. Make sure that your work is in an easy-to-use format and, above all, well photographed. You have probably 30 seconds to woo a curator – few have the time to go through endless images. Rather, create a short, meaningful impression by selecting ten of your best works to be professionally photographed than expect a curator/gallery owner to sift through '87 of my favourite works since my A levels'. Avoid using special effects that don't exist in the real artwork. Your CD should be clearly and memorably labelled, and accompanied by a list of the titles of works in the correct order, as well as prices, medium, sizes and year completed.

You could have to send out as many as 100 proposals to receive a single positive response. Not great odds you'll agree. (If though, after sending 100 proposals you have not had any positive responses, it may be time to review your work and change course.) I have always tried to not attach too much energy/expectation to proposals, trusting more that what needs to happen will. Some galleries may never bother to respond. That goes with the sending out proposals. Losing energy by getting angry will not achieve anything other than take your focus off your art. So set yourself the goal of sending out, say, 50 proposals (maybe five a day for ten days) and then go back to making your art.

How to approach a gallery

As we've heard, it's really best if you are able to wait for a gallery to 'find' you. But if you want to nudge the process along, these tips could prove invaluable.

- **Make an appointment**: I had been asked to bring work to a gallery out of town and Anthony decided to join me on the 90-minute drive there. At the last moment, he decided to bring some of his work along as well. After the gallery owner and his assistant had consigned my work in, Anthony brought in his. It was a disastrous move. The gallery had not heard of him and were put out by his sudden presentation of work. Had he called a few days earlier and given them his website details, he would have been in a far better position to ask if he could show some of his work to them.

  Gallery owners, particularly successful gallery owners, are busy people. Just strolling in off the street expecting them to drop everything and give you attention is extremely presumptuous. Even with the galleries I've now been working with for ten years, I still make an appointment. That way, I know I have a good chance of having their full attention, although it must be said if a client is about to make a large purchase they will understandably head in that direction!

- **Dress the part**: The Swiss artist Sylvie Fleury dresses in top-fashion names and radiates wealth and luxury. She presents these expensive labels as works of art and, through her dress, exhibits the concept that she herself is consumed by consumerism. An interesting approach.

  I was at a large gallery when a man walked in unexpectedly. He was dirty and unshaven and was clutching a scruffy portfolio of work. His image was one of self-pity and a hard life. Without excusing himself he thrust the work under the nose of the gallery owner. Now, this gallery (and many others in this league) often gets around 10–20 artists a week wanting to show their work. Before he had even opened his portfolio, this man had seriously jeopardized his chances. I'm not saying you need to wear Gucci, but smelling as high as a ten-day-old tin of dog food is not a great idea, and neither is clearly not valuing your work by presenting it badly.

- **Be professional**: To save cash when we were first starting out, we used to make our own stretchers and stretch and prime our own canvases. Restricted by budget, when I did not like what I had painted I would use the same canvas and paint over the first painting. I learnt the folly of my ways when a painting that had sold was returned to me by the gallery because the stretcher was badly made. When I sent it to be professionally stretched, the numerous layers of paint cracked and the work could not be sold. I lost a sale but learnt a valuable lesson, which a number of other artists have also had to learn: economize on your stretchers at your own peril.

Anthony taught me the absolute joy of destroying a canvas. When the painting has not worked, when painting over it will jeopardize the next painting, it's time to bring out the NT cutter and have a bit of slasher fun. Take your frustration and feel it disappear with each slash of the canvas. Then, feeling relaxed and calm, head for a clean-spanking-new canvas.

- **Be punctual**: If your appointment is for 11.00, be there at 11.00. It shows commitment and that you take both the gallery and your art seriously.

- **Be organized**: Have a list of the works you are bringing with you on hand, together with prices, medium and sizes. For easy reference, when presenting a CD of work, save the size, medium and artist's price as a caption on the jpg. Have your CV handy.

  Remember, once they have appreciated the value of your work, gallery owners are assessing whether they want to work with you. Being organized gives the owner the assurance that you will be easy to interact with.

- **Know what margins you are prepared to drop for cash upfront**: If you are fortunate enough to have a gallery offer to buy work from you upfront, be clear in your own mind what sort of cash incentive you are prepared to offer. If you hesitate and are unsure of yourself you may end up getting far less than you wanted.

- **Be cool with rejection**: Shouting abuse at the owner and insulting their other artists may make you feel better but is not going to help your career. I reminded a gallery owner of how about 14 years ago I had been rejected by her (of course, after all the other rejections, she had completely forgotten about it). Not taking it personally allowed me to go back to the same gallery at a later stage with different and better work, whereupon they accepted it immediately. Had I been rude on the first approach, I would have burnt my bridges.

- **Respect their viewpoint**: A gallery owner was often visited by an artist who would get verbally abusive about her choice of artists. He felt his work was better and minced no words about her poor artistic taste. His chance of achieving a place in her gallery? About zero. Another well-known artist with a drinking problem walked past a gallery owner to the fridge, helped himself to a bottle of wine and then, having consumed the contents, proceeded to insult another artist and the patrons. Also not a good idea.

  Curators or gallery owners know their market far better than you do. If they give you criticism, learn from it. Use the insight to grow yourself, rather than allowing it to extinguish your potential. Arguing is only going to close doors to you in the future. Remember: they may not see your work as a 'fit' for their gallery but another gallery might love it.

- **Create boundaries**: While you may become friends over time, your gallery owner is not your therapist. Calling them to pour your heart out at 3 am or expecting them to spend hours listening to your love life or financial woes is not what they are there for.

  Boundaries can work in your favour too, especially if you want to keep a professional distance. Question: what do gallery owners look for in new artists? Answer: good legs. (Yes, that really was the answer to that question by a particular gallery. Enough said!)

How *not* to deal with a gallery

> What I find annoying about prospective artists is when they don't research the gallery when seeking representation. Disloyalty to the gallery that represents the artist as well as a lack of knowledge of gallery requirements.
>
> ~ Margaret Campbell-Ryder, Red Hill Gallery

Here is a little list of 'don'ts' that might come in handy from Di Smith at G2 Art Gallery.

Don't:

- Present a CD with old work that has already been sold;

- Ask me what subject you should paint;

- Try and persuade me to take your work when it is clearly not suitable for the market;

- Present the work in a damaged frame, on torn paper, scuffed canvas and/or generally of a poor standard.

And more ways to irritate galleries from Laura Cole at Art at Five gallery:

> *The artist needs to give the gallery the time and space to sell their work and trust that they will be informed of any sales. Frequent visits and phone calls can distract the gallery staff from important tasks that allow sales to be made and the customer to remain the focus.*

The following tips may seem obvious but it's probably a good idea to swot up on them anyway!

- **DON'T consign work in on one day and then demand it back three days later because you've found a private buyer**: While most galleries are tolerant of your taking work back before the agreed time period, consigning work in and out before the agreed time will ruffle feathers.

- **DON'T arrive with wet paintings**: Arriving at a gallery frantically fanning wet paintings is sure to irritate.

- **DON'T arrive for an exhibition with work that has no hooks and expect the gallery to start drilling**: When I did a solo exhibition at the AVA it was a prerequisite to have all your work ready to hang.

- **DON'T waste time**: To the gallery owner you are one in a series of daily transactions. Unless they invite discussion, critiquing every other artist's work at length will simply annoy.

- **DON'T arrive unsure of your pricing**: Umming and aahing about what you should charge makes you look lightweight. If you are unsure, state your price, ask the gallery owner if they feel that the price is realistic and work from there. Different gallery owners will respond differently, and there are some that will try to deflate prices, hoping for lower price points. More established galleries should give you valuable feedback.

- **DON'T** arrive without your administration in order when delivering or collecting work. Have your consignment notes correct. The excuse 'but I'm an artist' doesn't hold sway.

How to overcome rejection

> *I admire all artists. It's the cruelest job you can take on, particularly if you are gifted, but forever unrecognized.*
> ~ Charles Saatchi

If we are afraid of being rejected, our fear manifests in two ways, neither of which are beneficial to us. The first is that we become arrogant in order to mask our fear. We develop a temperamental 'take it or leave it' approach. This may be cool if you are Hockney or Hirst. If you are not, then you may find galleries choose the 'leave it' option. The opposite side of the scale is that we become so afraid that we turn into mice and never move beyond our artistic hole in the wall.

As a writer and an artist, rejection has become a good friend of mine. It has to be that way. If I made every rejection into the message that 'I am worthless' and called each unfortunate encounter a 'failure', then chances are I would never have succeeded. So rejection has become my honest aide. It helps me see when my ideas are off track, when my technique is not as good as it should be, or when I am simply not producing good enough work. Without it, I may have wasted much time going down roads that led nowhere. It pushes me to reinvent myself and it encourages me to aim ever higher. The more feelers I put out into the world, the less I am attached to their results. If I had pinned all my hopes on one particular outcome, then chances are it would feel pretty rough if it didn't work out. If I have a number of options out there, then even if several don't work out it's not a big deal. And, if I am putting lots of fishing rods into the ocean, my chances of landing a big fish are infinitely greater!

Most writers and artists are rejected a number of times before their work is accepted (think J K Rowling, Wilbur Smith, Stephen King, William Golding, Manet, Whistler, Van Gogh and thousands more). Rejection is part of an artist's life – no matter how good you are, not everyone will like what you produce, the same way that people who like Dali don't necessarily like Degas. Accept, then, that on this path you will meet rejection. Also decide that it won't stop you from making your dream a reality. Remember that it's the work, not you, that is being rejected. People's taste in art differs widely, and because your work is not accepted does not mean that it has no merit. I have heard so many times of artists who have gone into a tailspin and refused to paint again after their work was criticized or rejected by a gallery. Just remember: the gallery owner moved on the moment you left. If you stop creating you are not punishing them in any way – you are punishing yourself.

The quicker you can let it go and move on the more your chance of succeeding. Repeat these to yourself when things don't appear to be going your way:

- *Failure is impossible.* (Susan B. Anthony)

- *The only real failure in life is not to be true to the best one knows.* (Buddha)

- *I'd rather be a failure at something I love than a success at something I hate.* (George Burns)

- *Failure is the condiment that gives success its flavour.* (Truman Capote)

- *Success is going from failure to failure without a loss of enthusiasm.* (Winston Churchill)

- *Most great people have attained their greatest success just one step beyond their greatest failure.* (Napoleon Hill)

The higher your self-esteem the easier you'll be able to deal with rejection, which is why building your self-esteem is so important. Rejection is simply a stepping stone on the path to success!

What you should expect from a gallery

These views are from Di Smith from G2 Art Gallery:

Artists should:

- expect clear and upfront disclosure from the gallery with regard to selling price (regardless of whether it is bought or on consignment);

- know the length of time the gallery will hold the work before wanting to return it;

- know how that gallery is going to market the work;

- receive a written consignment note from the gallery and keep accurate records themselves;

- understand the VAT implications on the sale price. There should not be VAT on the artist's portion (assuming the artist is not VAT registered);

- expect payment for sales within, at most, one month of the sale;

- expect their art to be on view in a gallery at (almost) all times, not at 'the back'; expect the gallery not to damage the artwork;

- treat the entire relationship as business, albeit a relaxed and generally informal business.

As I write this book, I am having an altercation with a gallery owner over non-payment for work sold. Ironically, when asked what an artist should look for in a gallery, she listed, 'honesty, integrity, hard work and fairness'!

Keeping track of your art

During the first three years of Anthony's life as an artist he estimates he lost in the region of 30 paintings – a considerable amount of money. Because his records were all over the place he wasn't able to say with certainty where what paintings were. Galleries – possibly intentionally, but more often unintentionally – can forget that they have sold your work. If you don't know where your paintings are, it's very easy for a couple of them to slip through the system unpaid.

Strangely enough, a few galleries have no real systems in place for keeping track of consigned work – perhaps naïvely believing that the artist will cover this aspect for them. The onus falls on the artist's shoulders to keep up to date with what paintings are where and how much they have been consigned for. Also bear in mind that if you are distributing two high-priced works a month, you'll have a lot less admin than if you are putting 10 lower-priced pieces into the market. As most people starting out don't command huge price tags, you'll have to produce more pieces in order to survive, resulting in more admin. In other words, you'll be pretty busy!

What's realistic? By the time I've photographed each piece, taken it into Photoshop, cropped it, numbered it, written the number on the actual work, updated my website, thought up ideas for clients, answered emails, sent invoices, got stuff ready for the bookkeeper, wrapped and packed art, altered my available work status on various websites, visited galleries, posted my monthly newsletter, stood in queues at the post office or filled in forms for the courier company, paid bills and checked payments, I've spent around 35% of my time doing admin.

No matter how good your admin is, though, you'll be lucky if don't suffer at least a few losses. A gallery started up in a popular seaside town and asked for my work. Because I had had no previous outlet in the area, I sent off some of my paintings. My work was selling well there but apparently things weren't going quite so well for all the artists. Only a couple of months after the gallery opened I received an email saying it was shutting down. The onus was now on me to retrieve my work. Needless to say, when I did get my work back (paying for the freight myself), a couple of pieces were missing and the owner had left town. So, if possible, feel out new galleries. Check out their way of consigning work. If it's left to you, or consists of a hastily handwritten piece of paper in an old invoice book, be wary!

I have heard of a number of cases where consigned work has been lost after galleries have gone bottom up. The liquidators step in and seize the premises and its contents – unless you can prove that the work actually belongs to you and not the gallery, it's in the liquidators' interests to keep it. Your word or a vague piece of paper with 'five paintings' written on it is not going to convince either the liquidators or lawyers.

A consignment note with relevant details, dated and signed by both parties is essential to keep accurate records. Figure 6.1 shows an example of a consignment note.

Joe Blog: Artist

1 Creative Road, Dream Park, 7777
Telephone numbers. Email address: www.joeblogart.co.uk

Joe Blog is not VAT registered

Consignment notice:

Gallery Name: Boma Gallery			Date: 19/10	
Artist Code:	Gallery Code:	Title:	Size	Price to Gallery:
(90-09)	Blog 207	Wacky Wally	500×700mm	£5000.00
Total				£5000.00

Your bank details here:

Terms and conditions: The artworks above have been consigned to the Gallery and remain the possession of the artist until fully paid for. Should they not be sold within . . . . . . days, the Gallery agrees to return them at the Gallery's cost, unless otherwise agreed upon. Payment to Joe Blog, the artist, must be made within ten working days of the painting having been sold and notification should be sent by SMS/email/fax of monies paid, together with notification as to which works have been sold. Paintings lent out to third parties will be at the risk of the Gallery and any such paintings damaged/lost will be invoiced to the Gallery.

I have received the following works in good order:

Gallery Owner/representative:

Signed at: Date:

Figure 6.1. An example consignment note

Figure 6.1 states things fairly clearly, although I am no lawyer (you may want to run this by one just to check if it covers you sufficiently). You should also cover the issue of copyright, to state that although the purchaser owns the actual artwork, they do not own the right to reproduce it in any form – this remains the sole right of the artist unless otherwise agreed upon. Some artists prefer to attach a copyright notification to the actual artwork (see Chapter 12).

Painting tracker

You will need your own painting tracking system, where you can see at a glance what galleries have what artworks listing their contact details. This is great if you get a private enquiry – you can easily direct clients to the galleries where a certain work is available. You can also keep track of sales by gallery so you know which ones are working for you and which ones aren't.

I run a programme on Excel which has a page for each gallery. Each page has their contact details and any other relevant information, work they have purchased and work they have on consignment. The final column is a list of work they may have returned, so I don't have the embarrassment of taking a returned piece back to the same gallery. This is invaluable information. I'm not a natural when it comes to bookkeeping but have learnt the hard way that avoiding this type of admin causes huge amount of stress when your memory fails you. I sit down several times a month and update my information, weighing this time up against the stress caused by poor management. Then I reward myself with a walk and a great cappuccino!

There are also a number of computer programmes being offered that allow you to upload images of your work and from there they get uploaded to your site, can automatically generate invoices containing the image, and let you see what works are at which galleries all in one smooth process with online support and pretty much all you need to keep your administration healthy. Of course they do need updating though.

7

Selling your work

'He's just good at marketing', I overheard one artist say to another, while discussing another artist's success. Many artists look down on marketing, refusing to acknowledge that getting your art seen and sold involves marketing whichever way you look at it. There is nothing noble in not being able to feed or clothe your children or yourself for that matter. Marketing is essential if you are to succeed. So either you have to do it (preferable) or you have to rely on your galleries to do it for you.

Why people buy art

If you are to understand your audience – and, yes, market to them – it's worth thinking about the reasons people buy art. Some of them are:

- as an investment;

- to create an atmosphere in their homes or offices;

- it mirrors an emotional experience to them;

- they are stimulated by a different viewpoint or visual approach;

- they like to be seen to be controversial;

- it expresses a religious/political ideal;

- it's reminiscent of a special place;

- it's aspirational;

- it has snob appeal;

- it matches their curtains;

- it's a gift;

- it mirrors what they want people to know about themselves;

- it makes them smile;

- they relate to the subject professionally;

- collecting art, particularly certain genres of art, is a hobby.

Ways of selling your work

Most sales of art are through galleries, auction houses, art agents and, more recently, at art fairs. Here are some of the benefits and pitfalls of the different channels.

Galleries

Galleries have the advantage of having an established clientele (if they have been in the business for some time), good areas to display work, good location (hopefully) and good working hours – often being open over weekends. Being in certain galleries enhances your credentials, making it easier for your work to sell. Yes, they do take a big cut, but they mostly have large overheads and many struggle to keep afloat.

Having a gallery handling the business aspect can be a huge advantage, particularly with clients who stall payments or who want to drive a hard bargain. By showcasing your work, galleries can often get commissions for you that you may otherwise not have got.

Chasing certain galleries for payment can be a problem. However, you'll start working out who does pay on time and who doesn't. The choice is then yours to do battle with the problem galleries or stick with those who do pay. That being said, there may be times when even the most reputable gallery is caught a little short and I have found that being accommodating for a couple of weeks can serve to cement your relationship in the future.

Sometimes galleries will buy your work outright, and although you may take a knock in your asking price, having the cash in hand saves you the hassle of follow-up admin. I have at times allowed galleries to swap a painting they have bought if they find it's not selling. This offer builds confidence.

A good gallery will give you advice and help build your career. When I do something new, I often take it to a few gallery owners whose opinion I respect. This has proved to be very useful in getting a feel for a new direction.

One gallery owner summed up my feeling when he said, 'I only work with good artists whom I like. Life is too short to do otherwise'. I guess one can reverse that viewpoint when dealing with galleries.

Having your own gallery

This was an option that Anthony and I considered. When an upmarket gallery in a great location came up for sale at a very reasonable price, we went into it quite seriously. Thankfully we talked ourselves out of it because:

1. One of us would have to work there as we could not afford additional staff.
2. We aren't good at selling and neither of us enjoys it. We both want to create art. Even if we were to take turns, we would become sales people – and working in the gallery would cause resentment.
3. Neither of us wanted to do our painting at the gallery. We are both messy and need large working areas. Being interrupted constantly by clients would drive us both nutty.

4. We did not want the pressure of covering considerable overhead costs each month.

5. Having other artists' work would involve administration over and above our own personal administration. We don't enjoy administration.

6. Sure, we could pocket the full price of our paintings sold, but we'd have to sell a lot of work to cover the costs of running the gallery and this probably wouldn't leave any time to paint, given that we also have children to look after.

If either of us had had a partner who would enjoy running a gallery it may have altered things. But we made what I believe was a good decision and left galleries to those who know and love the business – for which I am most grateful! Perhaps if we move to the country it may be an option to have a studio/gallery, but for the meantime I do what inspires me – create art!

Agents

Fancy the idea of devoting yourself solely to the job of painting while someone else carts your work around, hassles with galleries over payments, faces your rejections for you and is subject to the whims of clients?

An agent friend of mine was told to take one of her artist's works to a new restaurant for the owner to view. Problem was, the restaurant was up an elevator in a building where parking was difficult to come by. After carrying 16 huge paintings up stairs and elevators and through a busy restaurant, she waited for her client. Minutes turned into hours and still there was no sign of him. An SMS from his girlfriend informed her that they were 'running late'. Four hours and five cups of coffee had passed before the restaurant manager informed her that he would not be coming today but could she return the following day. The same scenario played itself out yet again before he finally arrived five hours late. He did buy four of the paintings but the story illustrates for artists the obvious advantages of having an agent.

Agents also get you into galleries and corporations where you may not have been able to get past the first phone call. A good agent will know just where your work will be best placed and will have the right connections to get your work on the walls. In the case of reputable agents, just being part of their stable is a good recommendation. An agent managed to get me into galleries who may never normally have taken my work but trusted the agent sufficiently to give it a try. When the works sold, it benefited the agent as well as myself and I was happy to pay for her services, particularly when that included my being paid upfront for all my work. Years later, however, when the agent still continued to rake off 25% for doing very little, the situation worked less well for me.

Agents are agents because they want to make money from you and the other artists they promote. This is fair enough: they have to earn a living as well. Art agents either demand a discount for the work in the region of 15–25% (but can also be as much as 30%) from the artist or they mark the work up from the artist's price, making it more expensive if they are selling on to galleries.

Most gallery owners dislike working with agents as they see them inflating the price of the work, making it harder for them to remain competitively priced. In reality, it's often the artist who takes a lower price for their work in order to fund the agent and still keep the painting priced the same as those not sold through an agent.

Many male artists seem to have the good fortune of having wives or partners who are willing to perform this task (I have yet to find the situation reversed!). If you have a partner willing to do this for you, then you're in luck – chances are they will promote you and only you, be passionate about what they are doing and keep a very watchful eye on the finances (for which they won't charge you 25% commission!).

Doing your own selling

Either because you can't get into galleries or because you resent paying their commission, or because you've been contacted directly by a client, some artists opt, at least in part, for selling direct. If you are working through galleries at the same time as doing your own selling, they may see you as competition. Be very wary of undercutting galleries.

Galleries don't exactly encourage artists to sell work directly. Understandably they feel that it undermines their business. Selling work at a large reduction only exacerbates the situation.

As a rule then, when selling direct I don't drop below about 10–15% of the gallery price. Some artists don't differentiate at all. It's tricky though because clients coming direct to artists do expect a discount.

Sometimes you may be asked to take work to clients' offices or homes to see if it works in the space or to let their colleagues give their input. I dread this scenario as invariably there is one person in the enthusiastic group who stands there stony faced – an instantaneous art connoisseur able to destroy what might have otherwise be a profitable transaction in seconds (unless, of course, you take the advice of a well-known landscape painter who told a student, 'Always knock a large hole in the wall while they are deciding. That way they'll have to buy the work in order to cover it up!').

Selling your work yourself can also be very time consuming. I was once asked by a company to go to their offices so they could see the work *in situ*. Four visits, numerous trips to and from the car park laden with work, a number of quotes and endless meetings later, I received a call telling me they had finally decided what they wanted. I waited with bated breath while they requested two prints. When they asked for a discount because they were purchasing 'volume' and if I would organize framing at a good price, I politely declined the opportunity of selling them a print. Nowadays, I am very wary about going to offices unless I am sure they mean business.

And then there are the couples. He loves it; she loathes it (or the other way round). Often this has less to do with the art and more to do with who doesn't want to max the credit card. The game can last for hours, even days, while the two battle it out. In one instance I sold a painting to a woman only to have her call in tears a day later begging me to take the work back because her husband was furious with her for purchasing it. I was happy to do so, but by that stage had left the town (where she'd bought it from me). Her husband was so determined to return the work that, on his next business trip, he drove 30 miles to my studio to return the work. In the end it's all about leaving the purchaser happy, and so when I've had prints damaged or changes of heart, I usually replace them in order to put a positive spin on our interaction if the purchase was recent. (I won't however 'swap' works out when a client decides they like a new style or a different concept, anymore than you can swap your car for a new one and not expect to pay in the difference.)

Selling direct you have to be prepared for strangers coming into your studio. I have had a couple of visitors who clearly had no intention of buying but were using the promise of a sale to snoop around, check out my studio, pick my brains ('How do you do this, and what paint do you use for that?') and examine my way of working. I felt quite violated by these visits and as a result now seldom take people into my studio if I don't know or feel comfortable with them.

Selling out of hand also involves quite a bit of admin – quoting, invoicing, packing (my worst!), checking payments, remembering three months later what you quoted when the client decides they do want to purchase, calling for courier quotes, dealing with couriers when paintings get delayed, generally accommodating clients' needs, having clients in your studio, and so on.

If all this leaves you cold, then maybe working through galleries is a good idea!

Trust *your* instincts too!

While many gallery owners and agents are highly knowledgeable about art, there are a number whose knowledge is limited to the artists they stock – meaning that not all good art gets into galleries and not all art in galleries is necessarily good. Yet so often as artists we do not trust our own instincts and wait to be told what's hot and what's not.

Years ago I was at a charity auction and a Paul du Toit painting came up for auction for £20. No one at my table had heard of the artist and so there were no bids. I loved the work. But £20 seemed a lot to pay for this unknown artist, being a struggling artist myself and so I did not bid. Nowadays, the work would be worth upwards of £8000. I wish I had listened to the instinct that told me this work was good!

8

Promoting your work

One artist, who had left his day job to concentrate on his art career, spent much of his time devising an elaborate website. Great – only, he was overlooking the most vital aspect of his endeavour. How was he going to get the people to view it?

Artists can be quite shy and retiring and many avoid public relations as it is seen as tainting the true nature of art. However, if you look at most well-known artists, there is a certain element of PR in their making. Emails, brochures, contacting your old pals in the media or winning a competition – all help to build art careers.

Ask yourself how you are going to let your target market know you exist. Exhibitions without PR won't get people there on the opening night, which means the exhibition won't be reviewed, which means the effort of making the art will largely be wasted. I'm not suggesting slashing all your works on opening night, getting publicly circumcised, making chocolate from your breast milk or crawling on your knees across the countryside (that has been sooo done, darling), but find ways of letting people know what you are doing. Then they can decide whether your work warrants forking out their hard-earned cash.

PR vs advertising

How do you get the best bang for your buck?

Basically, with advertising you pay for space in the media (in print, TV or radio) or for below-the-line mailing. With PR, you (or someone you hire) feed information to the media in the hope that they will find the story sufficiently interesting to write about or include in a TV or radio line-up.

Putting an advertisement in a publication can be costly, although in the correct media it does get you and your contact details into the public domain. I know of an artist who went all out and put monthly full-page adverts in a popular interior design magazine for a year. The paintings were similar in style so were easily recognizable from month to month. Reportedly it worked wonders for him and he battled to keep up with demand.

Unable to afford monthly exposure in a magazine, Anthony and I tried a quarter page each once. The only calls we received were from other magazines wanting to know if we wanted to place adverts with them. What I learnt from this is that regular exposure works, but once-off exposure probably doesn't. And of course, the 'product' must be suitable – to advertise in an interior decorating magazine you have to be producing interior-decorator-friendly art, which may not appeal to serious collectors and galleries.

PR, on the other hand, can be free or very economical. The most basic form of PR is 'spray and pray', in that you spray as much info as possible into the marketplace and then pray like hell it will work (although these days, professional PR companies have become more selective and more targeted). Even a small write-up and a picture of your latest achievement in your local newspaper can start to build your name as an artist. Community newspapers are always looking for local news and can be very obliging as a result.

I did a PR stint once. Actually, it was more for fun as far as I was concerned – sort of like performance art. At first I considered getting a sheep to paint for me and then creating a book featuring work by different sheep with a review waxing lyrical about each work as a way of having a dig at the critics. The idea got the thumbs down from my then agent in the UK. However the idea still appealed and so I called my friend Jenny, who owns a sheep farm. Her neighbour had a sheep that had been hand-raised and she asked the farmer if we could 'work' with his sheep. He agreed.

We christened the sheep 'Ewereka'. She was a very sweet animal, allowing me to stroke and even to hug her. Anthony devised a thick belt with a paintbrush holder which fitted comfortably around her waist. Then Anthony and I got together a canvas, some paints and brushes and a camera to help Ewereka create her masterpiece. We rested the canvases against the walls of her pen, so that the brushes made contact as she walked past. Armed with a handful of pellets and her milk bottle, I walked around the pen while she followed me and was rewarded with a couple of pellets or a drag on the bottle (she was completely oblivious to the art in the making; such was her focus on filling her stomach). From time to time we changed brushes and added another colour to the mix.

Actually, I was rather impressed with her creation. The following week I showed it to an art agent, introducing it as a new direction of mine. He was hesitant in his praise, but did say he felt it was considerably better than much of the abstract work being touted around town. Needless to say, he was considerably taken aback when I revealed the nature of the real artist (and did add that he had thought it was not up to my usual standard!). The media got hold of the story and ran a few articles on it, using the photographs taken by Anthony. This prompted an international media rights company requesting that their photographer come and re-shoot the 'artiste' in action.

That was amusing, because aside from me and the 'professional' photographer, two farmers (Ewereka's owner and Jenny's husband) came along to watch and assist. During the original shoot, Anthony and Jenny had got some wonderful pictures using available lighting and Ewereka's natural movements. The photographer, used to working with models, had some quite different requirements.

Holes in the roof where light came through had to be closed off, certain angles had to be maintained and a lengthy debate ensued over whether Ewereka should paint on a black or white canvas. 'Hold that pose there,' he boomed authoritatively at Ewereka, who took not the slightest notice as she chopped happily on her feed. Halfway through the shoot, Ewereka's pal, a black sheep, jumped over the wall of the pen to join her. The photographer loved this touch. But if professionally photographing one sheep was hard, with two sheep in the small pen it was mayhem. The farmers attempted to help, but were ordered out of the shed, which caused a bit of tension. Finally, after both sheep had gorged on pellets and milk, and realizing that the perfect picture was not going to happen, the photographer decided to head for a more natural setting outdoors.

Here, the rejected farmers watched intently as he led the sheep into a lush green field. Ewereka and her friend headed towards a far corner where a gentle hill gave way to a small stream, surrounded by deep, squelchy mud. As the photographer hopped after them, cameras bobbing up and down, both farmers smiled knowingly at each other. What the photographer didn't know was that this field belonged to Bacon, a particularly large pig who did not enjoy trespassers. As the photographer crouched low to get the perfect shot, Bacon made his way determinedly towards him. Full trot with his head down, Bacon ran straight into the photographer, sending both man and cameras flying. Muddied and defeated, he finally made his way up the hill, muttering that he thought he'd got enough shots for the day.

Neither farmer said anything as we climbed into the car, although their stifled laughter exploded into full-on guffaws as we drove off. The story was sold into some media in Europe as well as locally. Did it help sell paintings? I doubt it as Ewereka, rather than my work, was the prime focus. But it was a lot of fun and we donated the paintings to the local SPCA to auction. And perhaps it helped cement my image as the 'sheep artist'.

Artists Gilbert and George had the Advertising Standards Authority (ASA) questioning adverts for their exhibition entitled *The Naked Shit Pictures* after complaints had been received from the public. In the artworks they had depicted themselves naked alongside shit, presenting two taboos in one work. As the artists commented later when facing the ASA, nudity has been allowed in art throughout the ages and so there was nothing wrong there and, as far as they were concerned, the work was shit – the title was a fair reflection of the work. There were no charges and the exhibition was allowed to continue, although it caused a great media stir at the time and helped build their careers as 'living sculptures'.

Breaking the perception that nice people don't promote their work

Remember the old adage of 'one third talent, one third promotion and one third hard work'? If you are one of the many artists who feel that PR or advertising is somehow tainted, then rather think of PR as communication. As an artist you are in the business of communication, whether you realize it or not. Each work you do attempts to communicate a message to the viewer. Letting the would-be viewer know you exist is an extension of this communication.

I was invited to the Florence Biennale, where there were over 840 artists from 76 countries, each hoping to be noticed. Different artists had devised different ways of keeping their work alive in the minds of the viewers. One artist's business card had an image of a cow on it, and a battery-operated mooing device. Great fun, but would people connect it with her work? Others had produced leaflets, post cards and business cards, which flooded the small tables each artist was allocated for the purpose. One artist, being short of a buck, was selling his business cards! Believing Europe to be a place of honour and trust, I left a pile of my books at my stand with a box for payment and the price indicated. It worked well for the first few days, but alas on the second last day the books disappeared and so did the box and cash!

Not wanting to ship three canvasses of approximately 1500×2500mm home with me, on the second-last day I put a 'For Sale' notice on the pieces, along with my cell number, and left to discover the delights of Florence. An hour later my phone ran with an interested buyer. I sprinted back to Fortezza da Basso, where the event was being held. After a lot of heavy negotiating I sold all three pieces – admittedly not for their asking price, but it helped pay for the adventure! (Plus, I had damaged one of them when I spilt pen ink over it and the purchaser just happened to be an art restorer. So all ended well!)

Should you be going to an event like this, it's a good idea to leave a book for comments about your work with a column for an email address. That way you can increase your mailing list and set up a connection with interested parties.

Some PR/communication options

Hey, I'm still here!

It's a good idea to let galleries know what you are up to. This doesn't mean spamming them with every creation or idea you have. But sending them a sample of your top four pieces from the last two months keeps you top of mind and allows them to ask you to consign or buy pieces they fancy. It's a good idea, though, to get their permission to do this first.

In his book *Guerrilla Marketing*, Jay Conrad Levinson (2007) suggests that customers need to see an object 20 times before they will purchase it. Translate this to your work, and the more times a client sees your art, the more likely he is to purchase it.

Leaflets

It's not a bad idea to produce a small run of leaflets if you are planning to visit galleries, which you can hand out and to which they can refer if a client is looking for a particular style. They are also handy to give out at shows and so on. Make sure that you use decent quality paper, that the work is well photographed and that the layout complements your work. Also allow for a very brief CV or artist's statement.

Entering competitions

This is a great way to start building your art career and getting a bit of free PR. Even if you don't win the prize, you'll be interacting with other artists, picking their brains, finding out about local resources and hopefully getting good feedback on your work.

Don't put too much by the judges' decision – inevitably one group of judges will find some work more appealing than another group will. If you do win, that's great for your CV. If you don't, put it down to experience and move on.

The first time I entered three pieces of art (the maximum allowed) into an art competition, I won with one piece but the other two were rejected. I was hugely thrilled and next year hurried back to repeat the experience. That time I did not win, but all three of my works were selected to go on exhibit. I took this as seeing that my work had matured and was generally more acceptable. By the following year, I was a full-time artist and exhibiting in a number of galleries. That year, though, only one work was accepted. I was confused. Anthony experienced a similar course of events after winning the first year he entered. Had our art deteriorated? (I doubt it, as we were selling more than ever before and were more experienced.) Had the standard of work in general improved (possibly)? Or were the judges at the time not open to our genre of work? If it's your 15th year of being rejected then yes, maybe it's time to relook at your style of work. But if it's just a couple of times, glug back the wine at the opening, eat the soggy snacks, enjoy the art, congratulate the winners and know that at least a few more people know that your art exists.

Press releases

Getting press coverage in local newspapers is not as hard as you would expect. It's also free! Remember, though, that you are more likely to get coverage if your angle is newsworthy. Joe Blog having an exhibition of wildlife work is not going to get the media as fired up as 'Local artist invited to Miami exhibition'. You need to inspire the media to write about your work.

Solo/collaborative exhibitions

Even if you don't sell well at an exhibition (and many artists don't), having one of your own gives you a reason to create hype. By sending out invitations, emails and press releases, you keep your name top of mind. And should you get a review, even if it's not complimentary, it creates further awareness of your work.

Juried exhibitions

These are exhibitions where work is selected. Yes, applying may mean rejection, but acceptance looks great on your CV and also allows you potential to view other art, meet artists and get a feel for what's going on in the art world. These exhibitions often carry considerable media coverage. Remember, hiding your light under a bushel means you leave the rest of the world in darkness. Entrance is often free or nominal and, as they say, if you don't enter, you can't win!

Donating artwork

Galleries and NGOs often request work for charity. Whether it's painting a mini painting, doing an artwork on a wooden wine bottle (both of which I've been asked to do) or simply donating a piece, it's a way of contributing to society. While the media spinoff is usually not great and sometimes non-existent, it's fun and it feels good to be helping. I did a number of pieces for some prominent (and I mean VERY prominent) businesspeople who were involved with a charity. I earned little financially, but when the main entertainment at the gala evening let them down at the last minute, they handed out my paintings in order to create some diversion. The result was much laughter and huge acclaim for the work, as well as a commission. Even without the order, being told that the work had saved the day was great PR and a personal boost.

The other day I was asked to create four complimentary pieces of artwork to appear on nametags for a TedX event. Every participant walking around with an image of my work on their lapel is a great way to create interest and awareness, even if no sales result – and this came about simply because the original selected artist had let them down at the last moment. Point is, if an opportunity comes along, take it – you never know where it may lead.

Advertising

Certain overseas art magazines have sections where you can buy a small advert showing a piece of your work and your contact details. A lot depends on your work and its ability to read well in a mini size. It does seem expensive, but if you get a couple of requests as a result it may be worth it. Your website though will need to be up-to-date and impressive.

9

Using the internet to promote your work and create sales

Twenty years ago, the idea of selling art from a computer was about as convincing as winning the lottery. As artists and galleries started creating websites, this perception began to shift. Particularly with re-sales (people who have already bought an artist's work), sales via the web are increasing rapidly. To accommodate this, online galleries have sprung up worldwide, some of which are free and others of which charge a fee to exhibit. The Saatchi online gallery (Saatchi Online) is extremely comprehensive: you can upload your work for free, enter bimonthly competitions (the winners get put in a 'real' gallery exhibition), buy art, create your own artwork, vote in the competition, read up on newsworthy events and a host of other art-related interests – all from the comfort of your home.

To benefit from the potential worldwide exposure, you might want to design a website. The point is, though, will the time, effort and money you spend creating it be financially worthwhile? Having a great-looking website may impress your pals, but how will you start getting hits and converting hits into sales?

Developers advise that one third of the budget for a website should be devoted to creating it, a third to developing it and the remainder for updating it regularly (though many artists pour 100% of their money into creating it . . .). At one time artists believed that having a website meant automatic sales without gallery mark-ups. However, this has turned out not to be the case, since most clients want to see actual work or at least other 'real' examples of the artist's work before they purchase. That being the case, websites can have two basic functions:

- to let those interested view a range of your work, and

- to actually sell your work.

Many artists are happy for their sites simply to be a showcase – Anthony is a case in point. Initially, he tried to sell through his site. But no sooner would he update his site with available work than he would sell the work and the site would be outdated. To stay on top of things, he either had to update his site even more regularly, or he had to keep a stash of work for his site only. (Online galleries don't take kindly to your having work advertised when it is actually not available – understandably, as this irritates clients and loses sales and their credibility.) As he struggles to stay up to date with commissions as it is, this seemed pointless, and so a showcase-only site suits him well.

I, on the other hand, have found my site a great way to sell anything from books to prints, as well as paintings. I have also received an invitation to exhibit at a London gallery (which was genuine!) as a result of my website.

Online galleries and auction sites

Entire books have been written about marketing and selling art via the web, and stories abound of artists who have found a worldwide following via the internet. It is, however, not always so easy. Take the case of a South African artist whose work was requested by an online gallery in the UK. On their site they claimed to be able to deliver art worldwide to their customers within seven days. Because they were sceptical of delivering on this promise if the art was sent from South Africa (or New Zealand and Australia), they insisted the work be sent from the UK. They asked the artist to ship the required pieces to the UK where they would house them to until they were bought. Six weeks after the artist had paid for the shipping, they informed him that they had had a major change in direction and were looking for different art styles – and now they wanted the art collected. Not an easy task considering not just the expense and admin of dealing with freight companies, but also trying to persuade the online gallery to package and hand over from their side. Luckily, the artist eventually found another UK gallery who wanted his work.

Online auction sites are also touted as ways to sell art, although more often in the lower price range. Some online sites, such as Discovered Artists (USA based), started off by offering free exposure to a select group of artists while they built their company, with the understanding that after a certain period of time they would start charging. While there are sites that have a strict selection process, others allow pretty much everybody to sign up. Some charge for being on their sites, others do not. Obviously, for those who charge, getting as many artists to sign up is the focus, as they've created an income even if no work sells. Sometimes they charge no commission for sales, while others charge a lesser or sliding-scale rate, depending on how much you pay to be on the site, offering 'packages' depending on exposure frequency, number of works displayed and so on. Others do not charge you to sign up but work purely on a commission basis.

Then there are the online galleries offering 'juried' exhibitions. Pay an entry fee and if your work is selected you get exposure on the site. These are somewhat suspect as you have no way of knowing whether there is actually a selection process or if it's simply a matter of encouraging as many artists as possible to enter (and part with their cash to do so).

Just as there are numerous companies making huge amounts offering self-publishing facilities to rejected authors, the same is true in the art world. If it is true that only 1 in 1000 manuscripts gets published commercially, then it stands to reason that there are 999 authors desperate to see their words in print (and many unscrupulous people wanting to cash in on that need). Be wary of signing your life and your cash away. Just today we received an invite to an exhibition in Serbia – it's a proper hard-copy invite, received in the post, which looks legitimate. However, the gallery name that appears is the same as one in Montenegro which did turn out to be a scam last year. So, if it's not an unknown email sender informing you that they want to be your new best buddy, or telling you they want help with getting several million pounds out of the country, friendly folk posing as your bank, 'Peter McWealth' informing you that you are the only heir to a wealthy estate or the Italian lotto announcing your winning ticket, there'll be some supposed galley/art publication desperate for your brilliance to shine from their cyber walls (for a hefty non-refundable fee, naturally).

Regular galleries baulk at the concept of online galleries accepting any artists who can type their name into the submission box, stating that the online gallery has not seen the work and has no idea what it is their client is actually going to receive. One can only deduce that if the clients are receiving art they are not pleased with, they will return it, making the site unprofitable and causing its eventual closure. Presumably, this is all in the nature of the online gallery business.

I've also recently received a request from a website whose normal price at the time this book was being written, was roughly £100 to sign up and a further £15 monthly to have work featured on their site. My understanding is that they don't sell your work as such, but refer their subscribers to your website. Rather than the number of hits they claimed on their site, I'm more interested in how many sales have resulted.

The trouble with many online gallery sites who take thousands of artists without selection, is that in no time the site becomes heavily laden, making wading through it an impossible and time-consuming nightmare, even with search engines. If you're included in this type of site, chances are you will be lost in the mass of artists. In a normal gallery that has a website, they may have only, say, 25 artists in their stable so each artist has a good chance of exposure.

Of course, the internet has also become host to outright scammers, whose sole objective is to flatter you and, while you bask in your glory, extricate your hard-earned cash. You can protect yourself by typing their name or the organization's name into Google followed by the word 'scam'. Instantly, artists from around the world can inform you as to whether you deserve such praise or if you are about to be stung. For more on art scams see Chapter 11.

Your website

If you are about to design a website, you'll need to decide what sort of site suits you. Basically, art websites can fall into three categories:

- **Friend's site**: Hey, this is me with my latest painting/boyfriend/ at a party/on holiday, etc.

- **Overview-of-my-work site**: This will give you an idea of what I do, but don't expect art on the site to be available as I don't update my site very often.

- **Buy-my-work site**: I SELL ART! Here are the prices, order forms, shopping carts and credit facilities, and I'll be checking it every three seconds.

If you already have one, examine your website and ask yourself what impression it gives. If you were a potential client, what does your site reveal? Does the background enhance or detract from the work? Is it easy and speedy to navigate? (Waiting ages for pics to download is frustrating.) Does the copy complement your work? Are your contact details easy to find? Is there information about you and your work, testimonials from satisfied clients and lists of commissions successfully undertaken? If the site was last updated 18 months ago, it might convey that you're not interested in art anymore and have moved on to something else. The crucial question is, does your website inspire confidence in your work?

Putting prices on your website

In the interests of transparency, I put prices on my site – until an overseas agent sent me an abrupt email asking me to stop doing it (the matter has since been resolved). Unwittingly, I was creating potential problems for overseas galleries whose prices were considerably higher than those on my site.

Galleries will claim that your prices should remain standard worldwide, which is impossible if you sell work in galleries around the world after you've paid the added costs of agents' commissions, crating, import duty and freighting costs. At the higher-priced end of the market, these costs are more easily absorbed. But at the lower-priced end, having a standard price for galleries worldwide doesn't make financial sense. Where it can work, though, is if you sell to individuals internationally, where your price remains standard, but they pay for the freighting and any bank charges/VAT/duty involved.

Interior decorators and art agents will often ask for discounts rather than mark up your prices (I have known them do both), which is fair enough. Anything from 10–25% seems to be the asking rate, depending on the volume of work.

By not putting prices on my site, I have found that some people are embarrassed to ask for prices and as a result I have lost sales – a bit like the POA (price on application) advertisements in the property section of the newspaper. But if they are serious, these purchasers will often go to galleries or their sites, where prices are listed, to get some idea of the cost of your work. So all is not lost!

Getting hits on your site

A benefit of being listed on other websites (such as online galleries) is that they often have links to your site, which helps shift you up the pages of Google. Reciprocal links do the same.

Some people might advocate buying email lists of art collectors, interior decorators, galleries and so on. Personally, I'm a little concerned about spamming the world and am not sure if people who have never heard of you would be inspired to visit your site. Sending postcards via snail mail with your web address and examples of your work may prove costly but generate more hits.

Most commercial sites ask for META tags for your art – words, titles and descriptions which help draw people to your site. Different words have different popularity: for example, 'abstract' would rate a lot higher than 'aardvark' (the word rating can differ from search engine to search engine).

I get a weekly email from Google listing the number of hits on my site for the previous week, pages visited, length spent on each page, countries the hits came from and whether the hits were as a result of a search engine, direct hits or a referring site. Studying the information gives me an idea of how people are finding me. Also, if I see a number of hits from countries where my work is unlikely to have ever been, I brace myself for a week of expanded spamming!

(Alternatively, ignore all of the above, name your site smuttysexart.com and wait for the hits!)

Keeping in touch with your clients and building your database

You've got the website, you update it regularly with your latest work and events, and yet you are getting twelve hits a year (and two of those are from your parents). What's going wrong?

Keep those who have bought or shown an interest in your work up to date with your latest events. A link from the newsletter to your site helps add to the site traffic and the more hits you get, the higher your page site gets. Search-engine optimization specialists will also help to tag your work to increase hits to your site. Frequent news postings also help raise your ranking. I opted for a blog-type site via Wordpress, simply so that readers could interact and add comments and ideas. It's easier to update and alter than programmes such as Dreamweaver (it does have certain limitations however).

It's a great idea to send out regular emails or newsletters, reinforcing the content of your website, and reminding people to visit it. I love it when people approach me and tell me how much they look forward to my emails. This accounts for the very low rate of 'unsubscribes' I receive. I try to keep the content as entertaining as possible and seldom do a 'hard sell'. And if it's entertaining or interesting enough, people forward it to their buddies.

There is still heaps I have to learn, but I do know this: growing your email list will create and improve awareness of your work and maybe even result in commissions, which (being direct) will earn you a greater income per work than if you had sold via a gallery. Try to obtain email addresses from interested parties, even those who don't actually buy. Be creative in thinking up ways of getting people to subscribe to your newsletter. Understandably, galleries are not too happy to pass on your contact details to clients, so that's generally not a good way of increasing your list.

When you do send out emails, make them interesting and quick to read, with links to articles rather than pasting an entire article on the email. One art store sends me monthly emails giving me tips on subjects such as 'How to paint trees'. Nice concept, but it would be far more effective in my opinion to have short topic headers with clicks to the articles, so that I don't have to scroll through the entire 15-page email to get to the content that interests me. Ideally your email should be readable in its entirety with no scrolling required.

Certain words, such as 'win' are sure to get your email rated as spam. Mail servers have built up lists of suspect words, which are given a number rating according to which emails are filtered. The lower your potential spam count, the greater your chances of being read. Any rating above 5 has a high spam threshold and may not be delivered. Together, the words 'exhibition' (0.6), 'gallery' (0.8), 'exciting' (0.6), 'free' (0.4) and 'painting' (1.2) = 3.6, which is still under the dangerous 5 level, but could cause your email to head into the junk mail in certain email programs. My bulk mail provider allows me to check my email for these spam words before I send it out. Check if your does as well.

Your newsletter

A 2006 study from *Guerrilla Marketing* by Jay Conrad Levinson (2007) (which, incidentally, is an excellent book to read about inexpensive ways of marketing your work) revealed that people respond to emails according to:

1. Products or services offered (54% of people)
2. Written copy (40% of people)
3. Subject line (35% of people)
4. Compelling offers (discounts, free shipping) (33% of people)

Keep your content short, intriguing and simple. Make your subject line as personal as possible so your clients know the email is from you. If you can personalize the title, even better, such as 'Simon, have a look at my latest work' or 'Sue, it took a while but I got there!' or 'Sharon, feedback required!'

Podcasting

If you have something to say about art, are doing performance art or can paint an entire picture in five minutes with your left toe, then podcasting (from 'iPod' and 'broadcasting') is a way of bringing people to your site. Podcasting, for the uninitiated, is distributing audio and video files over the internet. Making a video to upload can be free, and uploading it won't cost you anything either. If the content is funny, insightful or teaches something of interest, you can have people around the globe watching it and hopefully linking from there onto your site. Remember Susan Boyle, the unknown singer on the TV show 'Britain's Got Talent'? Just one of her YouTube podcasts had 50,703,273 hits at the time of writing this book.

On 28 September 2004 there were 24 hits on Google for the word 'podcast'. Just two days later that number had risen to 526. On 2 October, there were 2750 hits. Thereafter, the number doubled every couple of days. By 18 October, 100 million hits were recorded. That's pretty awesome growth!

All you need is a digital video camera with a microphone, a computer and editing software (although this is not 100% essential). PodcastTools.com will teach you how to go about the process and you can download a free editing package from, among others, audacity.sourceforge.net. Your ten-year-old kid/brother will probably know what's cutting, even if it seems tricky to you!

The thing I've learnt about podcasts is KISS (Keep It Short and Simple). Five minutes is ideal. Anything longer becomes cumbersome to download and potentially boring to watch.

While podcasting your work in an entertaining or educational form may not lead to instant sales, it does increase communication and enhance your relationship with potential clients. I am currently animating a 30-second programme of my sheep to post on YouTube (EweTube?). This is not going to make me money as such and, given the time and the close to 500 frames I am having to draw, it might seem like an insane waste of time. However, if it's well received and recommended, I could have many people hit my site who would otherwise never have heard of me. Once there, they may be inspired to buy a print or two. Even if they don't, it still creates awareness far beyond the reach of an exhibition in my local gallery.

Other options

Use sites such as Facebook, Twitter, Plaxo and others to create profiles of yourself and your work. Each time you update work, you can send out information to those linked to yourself. Encourage your clients to become your friends/follow you on these media. That way, when you sell them an artwork you can upload it so all of their friends will see what they have bought and hopefully follow suit.

The educated customer

In days gone by, your client would have walked into a gallery, fallen in love with a piece and emerged with it tucked under their arm. These days, chances are your client would have gone onto several sites showcasing your work, seen your work in galleries (hopefully) and then looked for the best value for the type of piece they want. He or she can compare your prices across real and virtual galleries with those on your own site.

Times have changed but let's hope there's still room for impulse buying in all of this!

10

How much is it worth?

Pricing

You've completed the work. The gallery wants it. Now, what price are you going to ask for it?

I came from a freelance advertising and alternative therapy background, both of which charged an hourly rate. I wasn't sure what to charge when I started in the business of being an artist, so I applied the system I was familiar with. I thought about what was a fair hourly rate, and then added my cost of materials to reach the final price I charged to galleries.

This became problematic when works of the same size started differing in price according to the time I'd spent. So I created a standard price list based on size. The upside of this strategy is that galleries know how the pricing works and that makes invoicing easier. The downside is that you start getting to a sort of price-per-centimetre situation, which doesn't address quality.

Some of an artist's works are simply better than others and I feel the price should reflect this. So even though there are two 900×700mm paintings by the same artist, in my opinion price should differ according to the quality of each piece. This, however, is subjective and makes the paperwork more difficult. (For my own art, same-sized pieces are of similar quality so I've opted for the price-per-size option, while Anthony is opting for qualitative pricing.)

What my first system did not take into account was the other costs of running an art business, such as rental, petrol, telephone, internet connection, electricity and so on. Whichever method of pricing you use, don't forget to add up these monthly expenses and then divide them across the number of works you create in a month. That will give you an idea of what you need to charge.

Also bear in mind that certain galleries have price levels beyond which they believe they cannot sell. They may try to persuade you to drop your prices to meet their needs. This causes problems with other galleries where your work may have a higher price tag. So, do you charge all galleries a set amount, with the end price depending to their mark-up? Or do you set the end price and then deduct their mark-up, so that your profit varies from gallery to gallery but your end price is standard? You will have to address these issues in your own context.

Artists very often swing from undervaluing their work to overvaluing it. Inflating the price can indicate an inflated ego, while asking too little devalues the self. In the end, though, art obeys the rules of supply and demand. If commissions are flowing in and you are battling to keep up with the demand, it's time to increase your prices. If the opposite is true, you may need to decrease your prices to be more competitive.

One popular well-known artist was persuaded by a gallery to dramatically increase the price of his works. Seeing his works rise in price, his patrons rushed in to buy more work before prices rose even more. The result was by increasing his prices, he increased demand! In his case, because of his popularity, the gamble worked. I have also seen an artist go from asking just over £100 for his work to upwards of £2000 within a matter of months. The reason? He was approached by a European agent who hyped up the value of his work in Europe. This affirmation created excitement locally, together with greater demand for his work – and a justified increase. If, however, you are starting off in the art world and have sold only a couple of pieces, then this may not be the right road to take initially.

Galleries themselves are often good indicators of what prices they believe your work deserves. But do your research. Take time to tour around various galleries.

Discounts

Certain galleries almost always ask for discounts, claiming their clients demand them. If someone is painting my house and gives me a quote, I would not ask for a discount, neither would I stroll into a supermarket and ask for a reduction on the biscuits because I was buying more than one packet. Yet this practice has become acceptable in the art world.

If a client is buying more than three pieces of work, then I am inclined to comply. Likewise with galleries, but then I insist on payment within a week. Nowadays, though, I limit this discount to a maximum of 10%. If someone really wants the work, they will pay the asking price. If they decline, then I avoid feeling resentful for having let the work go below its worth. If galleries are buying the work from me as opposed to consigning it, I feel their belief in the work is worth a discount in the 10–15% region. Initially I was so thrilled to be earning cash upfront that I gave as much as a 30% discount. It was a foolish act and did not do me or my work any favours.

Another way some artists work is to only sell to galleries for cash. Should the gallery insist upon consignment, then they add on an additional amount. This forces the gallery's hand in buying the work. Unless you are a popular, established artist in high demand, few galleries will be interested in this option.

Clients coming directly to your studio can also expect some kind of discount. This puts you in a tricky position. If you are intending to sell directly and through galleries, be warned: don't undercut the galleries to the point that their prices look silly. They will get extremely annoyed, and you'll basically be killing your own market. Initially, Anthony was not clued up to this fact and sold a piece for what he would have given it on consignment to a gallery. The client who purchased this work had bought a similar work of Anthony's from a gallery a couple of weeks previously. He hotfooted it to the gallery and complained about how much more expensive his purchase from them had been. The gallery owner was not amused.

Some artists charge the same for work as the galleries charge (which makes the galleries happy), although this is tricky as different galleries may have different mark-ups. You can, however, stick to a rule along the lines of: gallery consignment price plus 70 or 80% (£1000 + £700–£800). This still makes you cheaper than the galleries, but not ridiculously so. Once again though the higher the price of the work, the less commission/mark-up percentage the galleries take.

Working backwards

Another way of working with prices is to start at a point that says: I require x pounds annually. That equates to x pounds monthly. My work sells currently for x pounds. After expenses I earn an average of x pounds per painting. To meet my target, I need to sell x paintings a month.

If you need to produce 10 paintings a month and you are currently producing two, then you will then have to ask more per painting. Be very clear and realistic as to how you will achieve the figure you require to live comfortably.

Annual increases

Each year material costs increase, irrespective of recessions and the general up- and downturns in the economy. If your prices remain standard year in and year out, your earnings are decreasing. Also, people often buy art as an investment. If your shares in the stock market are not budging in value year in and year out, your perception is that your investment wasn't particularly good. If your work is selling well, then annual price increases are acceptable – and often essential to your career.

'Artistic inflation' worked well for this established artist – wanting to increase demand for his work, he withdrew all his work from galleries for several months. Demand naturally increased as rumours abounded. When work became available again at a considerably higher price, galleries were only too happy to take it to fulfil the new demand and he'd pushed himself into a new price bracket!

Asking for payment

I don't enjoy begging galleries for money – I guess no one does – but at the same time, unfortunately, it sometimes goes with the territory in some cases. But I've done the work. It's sold. I deserve to be paid. Period.

Some artists really struggle with this aspect of their business, preferring to suffer rather than demand what is rightfully theirs. It seems baffling, but it happens. It's possible that if you scratch into the psyche of such a soul, you may find that asking for money equates to 'I don't have enough', which translates into 'I am not enough'. Asking for their payment is a reminder of feelings of inadequacy – unpleasant feelings which most of us would rather avoid.

If you recognize this pattern in yourself, you will need to work through it if you are to be successful in your goal to be an artist who lives comfortably from your work. If not, you'll be an artist who allows others to live off your work – and you'll carry anger and resentment as a result.

Money is simply a form of energy exchange. A PR person emailed me: would I swap a painting for free PR? One service for another. Money is the same: you've performed a service; you deserve compensation for that service.

11

Accepting commissions

To commission or not to commission?

Few artists are as happy about commissions as they are about selling finished work. The reason is simple: there is always an air of uncertainty in an unfinished work. Your idea of what the client wants and their idea may differ considerably. There is also the potential loss of control: clients may become too involved in the creation process, insisting on certain poses or colours, which may inhibit the artist's spontaneity or style.

Art is very subjective, which can prove challenging with commissions. A client recently asked Anthony for pieces for her home. He visited the house, took photographs and created a couple of small pieces which he photographed and then dropped into the pictures of the room using Photoshop to see which she liked the most. He was surprised when she described the piece entitled 'Calm Waters' as being 'too stormy' while she loved the tranquillity of another piece titled 'Approaching Storm'!

Commissioned work can be a potential minefield. A man commissioned a huge painting of his erotically posed wife. No sooner was the work complete than the man announced he was getting divorced and wanted to return the painting to the gallery – his new partner objecting to her predecessor eyeing her from above the bed. Since he was a good client, the gallery grudgingly agreed. The artist, wanting to maintain a good relationship with the gallery, returned his full payment in the understanding that he would be paid when the painting was resold. A year later, after the painting had not sold, the artist collected it and, deciding that he'd never liked the work, he slashed it, intending to reuse the stretcher. A week later the client contacted the gallery – he had decided that he did want the work after all and was furious when he was told it had been destroyed!

When an artist friend was still breaking into the market, she was commissioned to paint five dogs grouped in one large work. She spent a morning photographing the hounds and returned home with the task of painting five pitch-black dogs. According to the brief, each dog needed its individual personality to shine forth – which, given the mass of black fur, was no easy task. She returned a few weeks later with what I thought was a pretty good piece. The client rejected it outright and refused to even cover the costs, leaving the artist out of pocket financially and having wasted two weeks' working time (a good reason to ask for a deposit upfront).

My 'sheep' paintings consist of a red hill, a sheep and a title. I have received some weird commission enquiries, from masturbating sheep and castrated rams to requests to add company logos. In terms of lengthy requests though the following email wins hands down (I have changed some details to protect the man's privacy, and believe it or not, abbreviated it). This is a genuine request and I could not help being touched by the man's enthusiasm:

> *What is the possibility of a 300×300mm? I'm a bit worried that anything bigger would be just too big for the spot I have in mind. Well, here is the 'brief' for my Ewe of a different breed [referring to his wife]. I do appreciate your paintings being minimalist, but would appreciate a little bit more detail than usual.*
>
> *Title: Ewe watch it!*
>
> *Background: My wife always wanted a specific watch which she eventually managed to get. It is a rather big watch and quite rugged, which she promptly baptised 'GI Jane', as per the movie of the first lady to finish the Navy Seal course (very tough). (Everything in our house has names.) The watch's background is*

very much centred around flying, and their logo has a set of wings on it. Please see picture included of the watch with small wings in left top corner. Please watch (pardon the pun) the videoclip on the website, to get a better feeling for it.

She also loves handbags (leather, rugged – well used, wabi-sabi) and boots (leather, rugged – clean design as in horse-riding boot, not with bootlaces) in a natural to darker brownish colour (although she is still very much a lady!).

<u>*Elements to be included in the painting:*</u>

1) *Ewe (obliviously) with her big watch on leg, looking at it very intently,*

2) *Wearing a camo top and boots and maybe beret (?),*

3) *The name GI Jane subtly included somewhere,*

4) *With her rugged handbag,*

5) *The watch logo appearing in the sky,*

6) *Also 'time' (in numerals) raining down and stacking up on a heap, making Ewe look a bit perplexed (the watch is waterproof, so can handle the rain; also has fluorescent numerals so very visible at night),*

7) *Her birth date included somewhere (not blatant but as aesthetic element),*

8) *Obviously signed by you and indicated as '#1 of 1',*

9) *Decorated edges (as opposed to plain canvas edges),*

10) *Maybe the skyline can be a 'watermarked' with watch face as rising moon (?),*

11) *Your typical red-and-black scene.*

My Ewe loves the very rough, stuck-on painting technique, so you can really layer it on thick to create a 3D effect.

The watch is important – conveys her personality. She's done things most ladies haven't done, like a bodyguard course, advanced-driving course, driven big truck, rode big motorcycle, etc.

Most probably you'll need the bigger format for all this info, but I know my wife appreciates the simplicity of your paintings [my emphasis].

PS – Would a very rough sketch be possible so that I can picture it? Can do it on the back of the canvas, then scan and e-mail? Will make it unique – like the old art masters did underneath their paintings.

PPS – Thank you very much again

PPPS – My Ewe is a brunette with green-grey eyes (just for you to picture her better).

Remember that the requested size was 300×300mm and already had to include a sheep, a hill, a written title and my signature. When I suggested (a bit sarcastically which is not my usual nature) that a 2m×3m painting might be a better option, the man declined!

To date I have not charged extra for commissions, but am considering altering that policy should clients require specific painting themes. Conceiving ideas, sketching them and scanning them all takes time that I could have spent painting.

Like most artists, I request 50% non-refundable upfront deposit and the balance on completion. The main reason for this is if people change their minds I may be left with a work specific to an individual which I have little chance of selling. I keep my side of the deal by delivering on time.

Supporting the business

Open any brochure or magazine on upcoming exhibitions and it's enough to make one feel very intimidated – there are so many seriously good artists and, I used to believe, such a small buying market to support them.

As my work started to sell, I realized that this perception was faulty. Now I believe that the market itself is expanding as more.

More people in the world means more homes/offices/collectors. In recessionary times some investors look to other forms of investment other than the stock exchange and art is naturally one of them. Also, the more open we are to ideas of abundance (as opposed to scarcity), the more that perception of a vibrant buying market becomes our reality.

If you feel territorial about your work, you will be afraid to impart with any information and you'll see every other artist as a threat to your own survival. The more you withhold, the more you shut down the process.

However, the more you share your knowledge and skills, the more you open and expand the process. I am reminded of a fellow friend and artist, Jenny Merritt, who freely gives talks and imparts her knowledge to those willing to listen. When I asked her about this she was matter of fact, saying that as she imparted information and skills, she was opening up to receiving more herself. A sort of one hand-up, one hand-down system. She was not afraid to impart her knowledge because she knew that before others could catch and emulate her style, she would have moved on. This generosity of spirit as well as a determination to constantly shift herself out of her comfort zone has seen her become a successful artist well into her sixties.

If you are experiencing some success through your art, then support other artists by collecting work you love. This way, it won't only be the curators and patrons who end up making money from art, but you yourself can benefit. I have also occasionally swapped my work with another artist's, meaning we both benefit with no financial risk.

I know nothing about the stock exchange, but I have built up an appreciation for art. I consequently do not have to rely on others' opinions when it comes to purchasing. As one gallery owner said to me, 'Invest in art you love. Even if it's a supposedly good investment, I never hang art in my home I don't love'.

12

Potential pitfalls

Gallery sharks

The art world is a microcosm of the world itself, which has its share of dishonest dealers and untrustworthy characters. Most people you will meet are wonderful – but I have run into a few for which the same cannot be said. Without wanting to dwell on negatives, if this information helps you avoid such experiences, then it's worth including.

Sociopaths, according to Martha Stout in her book *The Sociopath Next Door* (2007), account for 4% of the population (that's one in every 25 people). What are they doing in a book on art, you might ask? The answer is simply that sociopaths prey on gullible people. Artists are often very trusting – we want the world to be a great place, so we trust people. We are also often longing for recognition and approval, which makes us easy game for the glib, charismatic charm and dishonest, manipulative ways of a sociopath.

Take the case of the charming, attractive woman who slid up to me at an exhibition and said she wanted my work – cash. I was flattered and enthusiastic about my good fortune and so when she had missed three appointments, I dropped in to see her. What I found was an empty gallery. There were the long stories about 'art being at another exhibition' and so on but every bone in my body told me to get out fast, which I did. I later heard that she owed huge amounts of money to both artists and agents for work she had sold and never paid for. I got off that one lightly. Once again, the lesson is: *before you deal with a gallery make calls to artists who have work there or ask around about their dealings.*

Then there was another young man who took many artists for a ride. He opened a large gallery in a popular mall and work flew off the shelves. The scammer asked for more work, promising huge payouts in the future. This was great. Until he ran out of excuses as to why the artists had not been paid. He disappeared into the gold-filled sunset, never to be heard of again.

Before you take more work to a gallery, make sure you've been paid for what has already sold. Try to get your paperwork as official as possible. Wording on a contract (see the consignment note in Chapter 6) will allow you some sort of protection.

Most con artists/sociopaths have no remorse or guilt. They feel clever for having conned stupid old you. They know the high cost of litigation will stop most artists from pursuing them. The good news is that few sociopaths ever succeed long term in the art business. Word spreads as quickly as their bad payments, and they gradually run out of artists to defraud.

Some art scams

Unfortunately, scams abound. This one happened to a friend of mine:

At a large fair, a seemingly wealthy client approached my friend wanting to purchase paintings for approximately £15,000. The client said he would pay electronically and collect the works the following day.

The artist received a text message the following day notifying him of the payment. All seemed well. However, he happened to have his laptop with him and on checking, saw no funds had come into his account. Not unduly alarmed, he reasoned that a transfer, particularly over a weekend, can take a few days to reflect, particularly if it's from a bank other than your own.

Later that day two men arrived to collect the work. The artist asked the security guards to accompany the men and check the vehicle's registration, which they did. As the security guards approached the truck, a man in the truck panicked and tried to escape. He, together with the two porters, were apprehended by the guards. Further investigation revealed that the same truck had been involved two weeks previously in an armed robbery. The text message was, of course, simply a false message created by the would-be art thief. As is so often the case, the main perpetrator and brains behind the scam were not caught – this time.

I've had my own run-ins with unscrupulous people. A well-known gallery owner got her assistant to contact me to ask me to pay half of an advert in a new art magazine. The deal was that I would get exposure, and she would get her gallery's contact details at the bottom of the advert. It seemed a good idea. The advert, she told me, would cost £1200, which we would split. What's more, I would not have to pay cash, but could send paintings to the value of £600 (wholesale price). She would sell these, and the £1200 gained by doubling the cost of the art would cover the cost of the advert for both of us.

I sent the paintings as agreed. Time passed and requests for copies of the advertisement were met with numerous promises and 'must have got lost in the post' excuses. It so happened that I was giving a talk on the radio when another artist, who had also been part of the deal, recognized me, obtained my details from the radio and gave me a call.

This artist alerted me to the fact that the advert had in fact cost only £400 per page and not the £1200 stated by the gallery. A further call to the magazine revealed that not only was this true, but due to the number of pages taken (eight), a discount per page of £80 had been given. By selling my and the other artists' paintings, the gallery owner would make £1200 per page, less the cost of £320 per advert, leaving her with a tidy profit of £880 per page (some artists had paid cash, which lessened the gallery's risk). With eight artists, the potential overall profit was £7040, plus paid exposure across eight pages!

Another scam was the enticing letter sent to an artist from an organization in Montenegro which was looking for work for its bi-annual 'Exhibition of International Nude Paintings'. The entry fee amounted to £50, which also covered a book of the event and only a 20% commission on works sold. The address seemed to check out and the work was sent. Needless to say, that was the last the artist heard until the paintings arrived back unopened, many months later, though the entry fee had long been banked.

Beware of emails promising you entry into art books with titles like *Artists and Geniuses* or *Masters of Creativity*. All you have to do is submit some jpegs, the email says. And then, in very small type, it says that if you are 'chosen' you get to be included in the book *for a mere £1000*. Unless you want the upgraded package: a double-page spread and a review of your work by some extremely famous person you've never heard of, which will cost considerably more.

If you have more cents than sense, then having your work published may be an indulgence to enjoy. Seeing your work in print will impress your friends and leaving it open on the appropriate page can't do any harm. If you expect serious acclaim, though, this may not be the way to go. Whole industries have built up focusing on artists who want to be recognized.

Another common scam involves the artist receiving an email from a 'client' in a foreign country wishing to purchase a work. The money is paid over except the 'client' pays extra because he wants the artist to purchase him a laptop as they are hard to come by in his country. There is always a rush or urgency in the transaction. The artist feels he has the money and so obliges, thinking he has nothing to lose. Problem is the payment was made by cheque and while the cheque initially may show up in the artist's account, it then bounces meaning that the artist has just paid for a laptop and lost a painting.

A self-confessed gigolo, according to his family, acquired a body of works purportedly painted by a deceased, little-known South African artist. He managed to dupe the Queen's art collection into purchasing several pieces from a Bonham's of London auction, giving credibility to the artist and prompting her work to fetch up to £15,000 at a later auction. Art websites around the globe started carrying information, posted by the man, claiming that her works were owned by people such as the Beckhams, Bill Clinton and Frank Sinatra and were hung in the Tate, Smithsonian and Rijksmuseum (the fraudster certainly went big!). Naturally, her work was neither in the galleries nor owned by these celebrities. He also claimed that she had been tutored by a number of well-known artists, none of whom, it turned out, had ever met her. The point is that it was relatively easy to 'create' an artist and her work, fictionalize a life history and get her work accepted in the highest of circles, thereby auctioning it at vastly inflated prices at one of the world's top auction houses (irrespective of the quality of the work).[1]

I received an email the other day, from a 'Lucy Courtney' working for *Lindsey and Richard Company* in Manila. The 'company' was apparently interested in some of my work for their stores and requested a website or a list of available work. Already my suspicions were raised, as most people access me via my website where I display available work, but decided to play along and sent a list. They ordered two paintings, requesting that I use their shipping/courier company and assuring me they would pay for the paintings with a credit card. This was odd – they hadn't even asked to see what the paintings looked like (they had ordered off the list which had no images) and no one in their right mind would do that, so my alarm bells were ringing loud and clear. But, there's always that 1% chance that they may have been genuine, so I replied sending them an invoice for credit card payment and insisting on a scanned image of the front and back of their credit card. (They could have obtained the number of another person's card that they might have stolen.) I also insisted that if they wanted to use their shipping company, that they paid them direct and not as they had requested.

This is where the scam was. I would be conned into paying shipping costs to a bogus company upfront and the payment to me would either not be made or would be fraudulent.

So be aware. These guys were pretty dumb; the next lot may be a lot smarter!

Be wary if you encounter some or all of the following:

1. The email sounds vague, such as 'we are interested in your work for our stores . . .'. Any would-be art buyer would know about you and your work and be more specific.

2. If they request using their couriers/freight company, unless they pay for them, don't.

3. If things seem fishy, insist on a back and front copy of their credit card. (They could still be fraudulent but this just makes it harder for them and chances are if they are not genuine they'll move on to easier prey.)

4. If they dangle large payment promises and seem in a rush to get the transaction happening.

5. They get angry and intimidating when you don't oblige their requests.

6. They don't ask you to send an image of the work they have just requested.

7. Sadly, certain countries get me worried upfront as we've had bad experiences in the past.

8. Don't be afraid to offend them with security questions – if they are genuine buyers they will understand your vulnerability.

9. If they appear to have overpaid you and then ask you to use the balance to buy something else to send with the work refuse to do so. Chances are the payment will bounce in a couple of days.

10. Check on where they first saw your work, what interested them about it and so on. If they can't answer these questions, then end the correspondence.

Scams can be small scale and local, or more ambitious in scope. For information on international scammers go to: www.artistsspace.org/ artscammerslist.html. This site lists email addresses of many would-be art scammers.

The gallery as a bank

While the majority of galleries are well run and professional, the few that aren't need to be highlighted in order to protect you, the artist. The less they can get away with bad practices, the less they'll be able to operate.

Some galleries blur your function as a supplier and as their personal overdraft facility. These galleries will take work on consignment, sell it (often not informing you that it has sold) and then they don't pay you. This is neither ethical nor justifiable and few artists are in a position to be able to afford this practice. Yet many artists allow this to continue.

I had not heard from one gallery I worked with for eleven months. I decided to call, saying that I would visit that week to exchange work. Surprise, surprise, I was informed that three pieces had 'gone out on approval' that very day. A follow-up call and I was told the work had indeed sold. A bit suspicious? Nothing in eleven months and then three sales in a single day? It could have been a coincidence – except that it was seven months before I contacted the gallery again. And guess what? Two pieces had 'just gone out on approval'. Then it happened a third time a year later . . . it was clear the gallery was selling work, not informing the artist and holding on to the cash.

Some excuses I've got for not being paid include:

- 'Even though your work has sold, sales have been down so I can't pay you.'

- 'I put a new lighting system into the gallery.'

- 'My bank cap has been reached for the month.'

- 'I'm too busy.'

- 'My priority is to sell paintings. Paying the artist is a less of a priority.'

- 'I have staff to pay.'

- 'I'll sort it out when I get back from my six-week overseas holiday.'

- And the common but most infamous one: 'I'll pay you this week,' when they don't.

The truth is that without artists, there would be no galleries. The reverse is not true: artists *can* survive without galleries. So you do have the upper hand, even though galleries may like you to think otherwise. I must stress though that these unscrupulous galleries are in the minority and the majority of galleries are a pleasure to work with.

Relationships are built on respect and trust. If a gallery owner/curator inspires neither in you, grab your work and walk away. Support galleries who support you and leave the rest to their demise. Frankly, life is too short.

Note

1.   As reported in *The South African Art Times* and *The Paarl Post*.

13

Copyright and other legal stuff

In wanting to make a viable living from art, I became aware that there were many emulators but few originators in the art world. After watching the art world for more than 20 years I became aware of how many similar works would appear by different artists. If I was to succeed, I would need to create highly original works that would have a broad appeal. I've decided to take the advice of intellectual-property gurus Frederick Mostert and Don MacRobert in their book *From Edison to iPod* (2007) regarding copyrighting my work and ideas: 'My advice to you is simple: run like the blazes and beat your opponents to the post!'.

Artists often ignore copyrighting issues and may find that their work gets used without their permission on anything from curtain fabric, to wallpaper to prints. I have watched at art shows people openly walking around with cameras snapping away at whatever grabs them (I've even seen orange-robed monks do this!) in spite of notices requesting no photography. Most of the times these images will not get used beyond the viewers' interest, but chances are a few will 'inspire' artworks in foreign countries.

What is copyright?

So, you've created a unique body of work. Someone comes along and starts copying the basic principles of your work. What rights do you have?

The minute you create an original piece of work – be it a sculpture, drawing, engraving, photograph or painting – the *physical expression* of this work is copyrighted. This automatic copyright means that you don't have to do anything or comply with any procedures in order for the copyright to be activated. The work must have an element of 'creativity', that is to say, it must be sufficiently different from other works in order to qualify. (I can't copy someone else's work and then declare my work to be copyrighted.)

Under British law, the 1911 Act provides that an individual's work is automatically under copyright, by operation of law, as soon as it leaves his mind and is embodied in some physical form such as a painting. Once reduced to physical form, provided it is an original work (in the sense of not having been copied from an existing work), then copyright in it vests automatically in (i.e. is owned by) the artist – the person who put the concept into material form. There are exceptions to this rule, depending upon the nature of the work, if it was created in the course of employment. However, a 1988 Act states that if the work was created while the creator/artist was in the course of employment then the author's/creator's/artist's employer is the first owner of copyright.

Copyright comes into being on the day the work is created and lasts for 70 years after your death in the case of art in the UK. This figure can vary between countries. It's an exclusive right that embodies the intellectual content, but it is important to note that an idea cannot be copyrighted – it has to be in a tangible form.

Although this copyright exists automatically in the UK, in some countries it is only effective if your work has the word 'copyright' or a © appearing on it, together with your name and the year of creation. If you are planning on exporting, adding these to your creation is a good idea.

If another artist's work is suspiciously similar to yours, you should have a good case against them. However, dealing with lawyers can be costly. As the aggrieved party, you would have to weigh up the impact of the other artist's copy of your work on your earnings versus the cost of litigation. If your PR machine has worked well and if you are already established, then the majority of people will be aware of who is copying who, and credible gallery owners, serious collectors and investors will give your copycat a wide berth. This being the case, a recognized copycat artist is unlikely to have long-term future as an artist, because whatever work they produce will lack credibility.

What are my rights (if any) on resales?

In the case of artistic works, on 14 February 2006 a new intellectual property right known as Artist's Resale Right was created in the UK. As long as you own copyright right to the work, under certain conditions or 'qualifying sales', the artist is entitled to a royalty on their work when it is resold. But in order for an artist to receive this royalty the sale has to be made by a qualifying individual or a qualifying body. The right only covers original works or those works where a limited number of copies have been made under the direction of the artist. It is a complex matter and there are restrictions on the price of the work, so if you feel any of your work may fall into this category, it's best to consult a lawyer who can fill you in on the finer details and explain your rights to you.

What about prints?

Your copyright is an exclusive right that allows you to use your work in all manners in which you can for gain or profit. Even if you sell an artwork, the copyright remains with you, the artist. Without your permission, no one else can reproduce or adapt your work, even if they own the original (the exception to this would be if you created the work for an employer who would then, in all likelihood, own the rights to that work).

I have been asked by clients for permission to use work purchased from me in their newsletters, cards and so on and have given permission provided I receive acknowledgement and my website appears. That way I open the doors to new potential purchasers.

Proving the date of creation

When someone was copying my work, the lawyer I approached, referred to the work as being 'confusingly similar'. If I wanted to litigate, the style I use would have to be identified as belonging to myself and then it would need to be proved that the copied style was causing confusion in the marketplace and as a result adversely affecting my sales. He gave me an indication of the costs that would be involved in bringing the matter to court. I reasoned that the financial costs were far greater than the effect her work was having on my sales and so decided to drop the proceedings (luckily she stopped painting and left the country to become a missionary – no seriously!!).

If you ever were to tackle another artist whose work resembles yours too closely, you would need to be able to prove that you were first to have created it. Proof of this is essential, so it's a good idea to date and sign each work on the back. You can even go so far as to write something along the lines of:

I [your name] confirm that I have created this original artwork on [date] which is copyright ©. All rights are reserved.

Add your signature at the end.

It's also good to have copies of the places where your work has been published. Dates of creation are available on websites, and books have dates of publication. Other records can also prove your case: leaflets, consignment notes from galleries (with dates), and the digital photos you have taken of your work (saved on your computer with the creation date). Some galleries give clients certificates of authenticity (with the name of the work and year of creation), although a certificate alone will seldom be enough to determine your rights as forgeries abound in the art world.

If you have something distinctive about your work (in my case, sheep), it is possible to get that copyrighted as it falls under a trademark. Just as you can't put the Coca-Cola logo on your company letterhead, neither can you put my sheep anywhere without breaking the trademark copyright law. Trademark copyright can include words, symbols and, more recently, rights of publicity, such as faces, names, signatures or endorsements as well as the trademark qualities of artists' work and overall impression of the work. It must be noted though that you can't copyright a style (so no one person can copyright pop art, for instance), colour usage or perspective. The 'feel' of the work is subject to trademark protection if it's deemed to be confusingly similar.

Protecting your art on the web

The previously mentioned artist copied the style of my paintings, took an introduction line from my site (which had also been published in a book of mine) and, altering a few words, pasted the copy on her own website. Underneath it, in huge type, she added prominently: 'All artwork, copy and images on this website are copyright of the artist and may not be reproduced in any form without prior written permission by the artist'. I could not resist sending her an email asking her to which artist she was referring!

A few months ago at my stand at a show, I overheard one woman say to her friend, 'Choose the ones you like and then download them off her site and get them printed on canvas and have it stretched. That way it'll look like an original'.

So, is it possible to protect your work on the web? Go to Google images, type in the name of a professional artist you know and hundreds of images of their work will most likely appear – nice and easy to download and print at random even if they are a little low on resolution. The practice is illegal as the images are copyrighted, but can I really protect that copyright when it's infringed in Beijing, Beirut or even Bude? The answer, of course, is no.

The internet has allowed images to be spewed across the globe, making artists particularly vulnerable. The downside of the relative ease with which you access galleries, art information and so on is that your art and concepts can easily be copied. There are things you can try to protect your work. In programmes such as Photoshop you can put a watermark over your paintings. It's not completely foolproof as you can get rid of the watermark if you know your way around photo retouching, however, it is a deterrent. Pictures on the web are low resolution, which provides some protection, but there are programmes now that can increase resolution. What all this is saying is that for the determined copier, your efforts are probably wasted. It's simply a matter of individual conscience.

Does this mean you should be paranoid and not show any of your work on the internet? My feeling is no. Even if it is illegally downloaded, it's still not the original and having an original is still what everybody desires. If people are pinning prints of your work on their walls, it's still advertising and awareness for you.

Using logos in your art

Andy Warhol did not get legal approval from Campbell's soup when he produced his famous 1962 screen prints of their product. Should you get approval when using a Pepsi logo in your landscape? Companies don't generally make a habit out of suing artists, particularly if the work is a one-off. They can, however, get twitchy if you use their logo in an artwork from which you make prints or other products. Corporates tend to lose their sense of humour and artistic appreciation when you mess with their brands, especially if it's in a manner that doesn't favour their products, so be wary.

An original painting/artwork is seen as more of an act of freedom of expression than a T-shirt or postcard is. However, opinion can differ between lawyers, so before you start rolling out your artwork featuring well-known brands, get legal advice.

Insurance

Your hands are your income. So it's not a bad idea to have some form of insurance in case they are damaged. Many insurance companies put artists in the 'high-risk' category – perhaps suggesting that artists lead lives 'on the edge'. Consequently, insurance can be costly, but there are some firms who are happy to insure you. A good broker should be able to give you advice.

General

The information here is a guideline only. As with all things legal, when in doubt, seek professional advice.

14

Lessons I've learnt

Artists need to be loyal and have a good rapport with their represented gallery and have continuity of quality artwork. They also need to listen and take advice from the gallery curator.

~ Margaret Campbell-Ryder, Red Hill Gallery

Don't chop off your ears

Not all advice or criticism may be relevant – like your mum insisting you explore realistic still-lives in an attempt to stop you from doing the sex-subversion piece you are currently engaged with. However, ignoring the comments in a review or from various galleries owners may be at your own peril.

Learn from other artists. Go to exhibitions, read reviews, study books on art and art magazines. Take a trip to London to the Tate Modern and the many galleries that abound there. Go to Paris and the Pompidou, if you can afford to, travel and see art around the globe, or start with the gallery closest to your home. Expand your horizons. Listen, watch, learn and then find your own path.

Don't be afraid to change and explore

For most of us, change is about as thrilling as going to the dentist! We may like to *think* we embrace change, but just wait and see how thrilled we are when we have our carefully conceived plans altered.

This was very cleverly demonstrated at a lecture by international consciousness teacher and author Carolyn Myss. At a workshop of hers that I attended, people had booked months previously and arrived early to grab the front seats. At the beginning of her lecture, she asked those sitting in the front few rows of the hall to change seats with those sitting at the back. Many participants instantly became angry and attempted to retain their seats. The aim was to teach the participants just how hard change is and what emotions arose over a simple seating arrangement. So much for all of us who claim to embrace change – if keeping one's place at a lecture holds so much resistance, just imagine what *real* change can do!

Change is the very nature of life: everything in the universe is in a constant state of flux. To resist change is to attempt the impossible, like altering universal law. Our efforts will only use up huge amounts of energy and frustrate us in the process, so we might as well accept change as inevitable. We cannot control the universe.

How does art relate to change? Art is change. Why? Because the artist takes the raw material – paper, canvas, found objects, a block of wood – and transforms it into an object of beauty. The whole creative process is about change – that is why it can be threatening and why we can be terrified of a large, blank canvas. It's why we keep telling ourselves that we will explore our creativity, but we just don't ever seem to have the time, space, knowledge or tools to do so. When we realize this, we come to the understanding that we are the canvas and that we can choose to create with our lives whatever picture we choose. Then we become the masterpiece.

The more you are prepared to change, the more you can grow as an artist. The less we are dictated to by others' beliefs and the less motivated we are by the need for approval, the greater and faster our potential for change will be.

Picasso moved from his 'Blue Period' to the 'Rose Period', the 'African Influence' period, Cubism (Analytical and then Synthetic) and so on. Working the same way then is not going to get you to greatness. Push yourself firmly out of your comfort zone and explore the world around you.

Don't question your intuition

I wish I'd listened to my inner voice when it came to anything from dealing with galleries to choosing suppliers and buying investment artworks.

Don't skimp on materials

My first art teacher taught me a valuable lesson: if you use student materials, you will remain a student. Student paints are less expensive for a reason – they are cheaper to make and don't work as well. The cheap paints usually contain less pigment, making them harder to work with if you want a solid colour (particularly if you're working over a darker area with a lighter colour). I used to advise my pupils to rather buy a few tubes of better quality paint and mix the other colours they needed than a whole range of cheap paint that would only frustrate them.

As an art teacher, I was witness to the frustrated attempts of my pupils to paint on cheap canvases. With little or no absorption, the paint balanced on top, would not spread and generally never gave the outcome the artist was looking for.

However, there is a balance here. If you're doing huge Jim Dine-type works, then pure sable brushes aren't really a necessity! And don't let the price of things prevent you from starting on your artistic journey.

Realize that the green grass on the other side requires a mow

Are you one of the alleged 7% of people who can work happily on their own, or do you need a constant throng of people around you? Can you motivate yourself to work or do you need someone giving you orders? Many of us long to work from home . . . until you sit day after day chatting to the cat, feeling isolated, unmotivated and, on your umpteenth cup of coffee with no work done, longing for a bit of human interaction. You may feel a loss of power just when you believed your new role would empower you.

Interruptions from friends, family or your inbox can become a pleasant respite from wondering what to create. It's an aspect of an artist's life that is seldom considered while your buddies admire your freedom. My advice is to address your ability to self-motivate before you slide down the slippery slope towards depression. Ask yourself:

- Am I happy with my own company?

- Do I procrastinate when it comes to work? How can I work to solve this?

- Am I so motivated that I can create without deadlines or bosses?

- Can I challenge myself?

- Am I happy being out of my comfort zone?

- Have I demonstrated these abilities in the past?

Change your thinking

How can you shift from hoping you'll succeed to *knowing* you will?

During the period when we were neither art directors nor artists, I went to a transformative workshop. I felt really low and afraid at the time. People were surprised to meet this person who was an author and ex-director of an ad agency at such a low ebb. Somehow the knowledge gleaned over the years wasn't working very well for me.

At the end of the workshop the facilitator did an exercise where a word would come to each of us to inspire and uplift us. Imagine my confusion when the words that popped into my consciousness were 'no hope'.

I left the workshop in a seriously low place, wondering why I had invested the time and money in going. The words 'no hope' haunted me over the next few days, playing back at me like an irritating advertising jingle. Then it suddenly dawned on me. I was living my life *hoping* for some sort of miracle, the way one hopes to win the lottery or an all-expenses-paid luxury cruise. I was hoping my life would change without actively going through the steps to make it change. I had to reach the point of *knowing* that we could make a living from art as opposed to *hoping* that we could. Hoping comes from a disempowered space. Knowing comes from an empowered space. 'I know I can' carries a huge amount more potential than 'I hope I can'.

Suddenly I was immensely grateful, both for the workshop and facilitator and also for the message, which had shown me where I was going wrong. Basically, it was up to me to make things happen.

Focus and prioritise

> *Everybody lives according to their values, so what is most*
> *important to them is where they will be most focused,*
> *structured, energetic and interested.*
> *People are inspired if they do what they enjoy.*
> *Career fulfillment is fulfilling their vision every day.*
> ~ Dr John Demartini
> (*HR Future*, November 2008)

If your main interest is getting fit for a marathon, then that's where your energy will go, which means there is little left to go into your artistic goal.

How much do you want to succeed? What are you prepared to let go of to succeed? There is no wrong or right here. If all your money, time, thoughts, friends, personal space, conversation, dreams and inner dialogue revolve around music, then being a visual artist is unlikely to happen. The question is: is art the top of your list of priorities?

I still find myself not focusing on priorities and wandering down seemingly meaningless paths. Fortunately I have Anthony and friends who hall me back up onto the path.

Let go

Anthony taught me this lesson. If it's not working, trash it or slash it. Struggling with a work that's not happening just because of the cost of the canvas often causes more frustration than it's worth. Besides, slashing a canvas is a hugely fun thing to do!

And, finally, you can!

Any dream comes at a price. No goal is achieved without risk. Behind every great work of art are numerous less successful attempts. With a combination of loads of talent, drive and belief in yourself, you can make the dream of living as an artist your reality.

Remember: the fun is the journey, not just the destination.

Good luck!

Addendum

Questions and answers

Since the first copy of this book, I have received a number of questions from you the readers, as well as interesting questions from TV and radio interviewers, which I have attempted to answer to the best of my abilities/ experience. Other issues have emerged which I felt are worth including as well.

Here are some of those questions/issues.

Can commerce and creativity live together?

Q: (from a radio presenter) *Aren't you prostituting yourself by considering finance when you create art? As an artist, should you not be concentrating only on making art?*

A: Yes that is a common perception, but what one has to realize is that creating art while worrying about how you are going to pay the bills is in itself very creatively constricting. It's really weird but there is the perception that artists should be impoverished and that there is somehow a stigma with actually being paid for your work. In the corporate world people who are successful are highly rated, but somehow the minute you put art and business in the same sentence the feeling seems to be that this is not in keeping with the archetype of an artist.

(As the presenter carried on pushing the point, it occurred to me if she would have been doing the same were she interviewing an architect, plumber or an interior designer, in other words, questioning the tainting of art, with the word 'sell'. As if to sell made one less of a 'true' artist? In the days of patrons this could have applied but a bunch of starving artists means a bunch of people focused on the need to exist rather than the opportunity to create.)

To discount or not? That is the question

Q: *I have had work in my local gallery for some years now, but sales have now dropped off badly (the economy, I guess). Currently I have no other gallery through which to cycle the works. As the paintings are more than a year old, what are your thoughts on discounting/ marking down? I need the money, but what effect will this have on my 'image'?*

A: We were discussing mark-downs at a gallery the other day – a well-known artist has cut his prices by about 50%. My feeling is that this was not a good move and would severely upset people who have bought his work in the past for the higher price and would now feel cheated because it's worth so much less.

Doing so would also position him as an artist on his way down not up so would not inspire confidence from an investment point of view.

From your personal standpoint, it does rely naturally on how much work you have sold into the market – if its hundreds of pieces, then that's hundreds of people who are going to be miffed.

If only a few then perhaps it's not such a serious move. (There is also no guarantee that lowering the price of the work will lead to a sale, maybe the work lacks appeal, etc?)

Still, times are tough and you need to eat. So the way I felt is that it's best to hold one's prices but make it clear to the gallery that you would be prepared to negotiate if they felt that would swing the deal (this would also give you an idea if it's the money or the work that's a problem).

By allowing a margin of discount, the client feels they have got a good deal and your pricing/image remains intact. This does rely heavily on the integrity of the gallery to be honest about when they have sold work for less and when not.

Better move though, would be to find a few more galleries so you can shift works around. So often I've found a painting that has remained unsold, when moved to another gallery, suddenly sells.

I'm asked regularly (at least 14–20 times a year) to donate art to varies charities to auction. One charity this year came up with a new suggestion: they would take several of my works for auction and instead of just giving them away, as I normally do, they offered to pay me an agreed (albeit reduced) amount for each work – what they earned over and above that went to the charity. This was a great way of helping others and also helping me, as getting something was better than nothing. Win/win all round.

Gallery vs. direct pricing

Q: *What should I charge for work that I sell directly, in other words, not through galleries/agents, etc.?*

A: Galleries understandably do not like artists to sell directly to customers. However, it is going to happen and there is a win/win balance to be found, and being upfront with galleries initially, usually takes away from potential problems later on. Most galleries mostly do accept that there will be private sales. As one gallery owner put it, 'People will claw their way over the mountain by their toenails if they believe they can get your work cheaper on the other side'. A little extreme perhaps but in some cases may be true!

So, what to charge? In my experience I either charge the same price as the gallery is charging, or more commonly 10–20% less than the average gallery price for my work. It's a contentious issue though. However, this pricing allows clients to feel seeking me out has been worth the effort and I am not making the galleries look ridiculous price wise.

Nowadays when I'm working with a new gallery, I let them know upfront what my direct prices are and this openness avoids any misunderstanding at a later stage.

Two replies from other artists to the same question

Artist A: I have thought about this as well and have come to the conclusion that if people want to buy privately it is because they want to pay less. Times are tough and buyers do shop around! My guess would be somewhere in between, like 75% of the gallery price sounds reasonable enough.

Artist B: My attitude to this is if you seriously want as many outlets as possible for your work you shouldn't undercut the galleries. However, I am very careful about which galleries I put my work into. I ask lots of questions about how they intend to earn their commission. Galleries have overheads and part of their overheads, if they are doing their job properly are, advertising, previews, maintaining a customer database and making the most of it, contacting their clients when there is new work in the gallery, paying their artists on time and so on. Some galleries take the commission and do nothing. They don't get my work.

That being said, if I do get customers to my studio looking to buy cheaper than in the gallery *I do* offer discounts *if* the customer wants to make multiple purchases – two or more pieces with a discount on a sliding scale depending on how many they purchase.

Referral fees?

Q: *What about 'referral' fees if a client buys direct but came to me from a gallery?*

A: If a gallery has spent time and effort with a client and if the client first saw your work in their particular gallery, I am happy to pay the gallery a referral fee if I find out that the person then came to me afterwards as a result. (This does get tricky as with about 20 galleries stocking my work, it often happens that a would-be buyer has come across it several times before in different places.) This can be a problem though as in one instance I had two galleries both claiming a referral fee for the same contact, which meant there wasn't much left for me. These things are best discussed upfront with a gallery before the situation occurs so that there is no upset should it ever occur.

The amounts I've paid for referrals are usually between 10–20% of the amount I receive for the work, that is to say, not the galleries' normal amount because I usually have paid to wrap the work, taken the time to make the sale, charged them less than the gallery price and so on. In the instance where a gallery did not actually have any of my work, but simply when the clients asked after me, called me and gave me the enquirers' contact details, we settled on 10%. Where the gallery did have my work and went to more effort, we agreed on 20%.

Then there is the opposite argument that says if I refer a client to a particular gallery and they purchase a work of mine, do I get a referral fee from the gallery? (The same way they'd ask one of me?) I doubt they'd agree!

Art that doesn't sell?

Q: *My garage is piled high with works that didn't sell, what do you do with your old work?*

A: I'm sometimes tempted to trash a painting if it hasn't sold after a period of time. However, I have learnt 'The Law of Murphy' that says that no sooner have I taken an NT cutter to the work, that I get a request for it – this must have happened about 10 times. If I don't like the work, I will still destroy it, but work that just hasn't sold, I now store away any older works knowing that one day they will just click with someone. Anthony is the problem though – he trashes paintings that many times I feel are good works and could have sold. Still, it takes a lot to convince him of this sometimes . . .

Hard work = success (mostly)

This is not so much a question, but more of an omission perhaps in that Anthony made the point that nowhere in the book had I made mention of how hard most artists need to work to be successful. Sure you can structure your time (we just went stand-up paddle boarding with dolphins!) but there is seldom a weekend that we both aren't working at least some of the time and, often, most of the time. To produce enough art to live off usually requires a lot of hard work, so being an artist is NOT an easy option, in fact compared to my days in advertising it's a lot more work (it's just that the work is more enjoyable!).

Nickname or real name?

Q: *What are your views on her signing one's work with a nickname?*

A: Not sure why you'd want to do this, unless, like an author who writes in different genres uses a pseudonym, you want to clearly create a distinction between styles. There are some artists who do this – graffiti artists who want to avoid being caught, for example. If you are fortunate enough to become wildly famous, it could be confusing for the media I'm guessing. In the end don't know any rules as such. I guess it's up to the individual to decide.

I've been framed!

Q: *Should I frame my work or leave it unframed?*

A: Do you spend a lot of money and get your work framed, only to have the client request the painting sans frame? (This has happened to me several times and have been left with a frame that didn't really work on anything else.) Framing can be a personal issue based on the décor of the room the work is going to be hung in and the taste of the purchaser. To avoid the issue I, and many other artists, started using deeper stretchers – 5 to 10cms deep, meaning that framing was not needed. Given the cost of framing, this made sense.

Framing is expensive and will often add considerably to the cost of your painting, making it harder to attract a purchaser, it will however (if well framed) enhance the work, which will in turn make it more purchasable. So it's 50–50. Problem comes though, if the work doesn't sell and while you own the painting, the frame is theirs. It hasn't happened to date with us, but it's a possibility. However, even the most stunning frame won't compensate for a bad piece of art.

Many galleries will not accept unframed work and some have even offered to pay for the framing of our work themselves, recuperating their expense when the work sells.

If you are not going to frame do make your edges neat – either carry the painting around the sides, keep them clean (masking tape wrapped around the edges while you paint works well for this), or paint the edges a colour that works with the painting.

There are some more conservative galleries that won't take unframed work, so you may be forced to frame simply to get on the wall. Many of them have a sideline framing business and may offer a discount for the job (just be careful not to frame all your work for their profit, rather than your promotion).

For overseas clients, framing is usually a big no, as it adds considerably to transport costs and many not allow for the cheaper option of rolling your work. Personally, apart from watercolours, I avoid framing, leaving the client free to decide for themselves.

Rejection – the artists' lament

Q: *I'm tired and angry about being rejected by galleries and I sympathize with Van Gogh's ear-cutting escapade. (Presumably she felt he'd hacked his ear off from frustration with rejection.) I'm not sure what to do anymore to get my career to happen.*

A: My reply to the artist (abbreviated): having experienced rejection first hand, both through art and writing, it has become a familiar friend and one that pushes me out of my comfort zone to explore new directions.

I do understand your frustration and anger – it can be hard when you've put so much time and effort into something and it gets rejected.

The art and the writing worlds are hard nuts to crack.

Commercial galleries, as mentioned in the book, are for the most part, businesses who sell art rather than art lovers who have a business. If they know the work has been proven to sell/be of commercial value, then they want to cash in on that success. There's less risk with known/proven artists.

If the business has artists on board who are working for them, unless the art is really something completely new and exciting, the hassle of taking on another artist is not attractive. So to be accepted takes the 'wow' factor.

The galleries are not the enemy. They are businesses. It's simply a matter of can this sell or not? Do I need new art/artists now?

Sometimes they naturally do get it wrong, but most of them are still in business because they know what their market wants. (It's no different in the writing world where there are thousands of books written about, let's say, yoga. To get another book published on yoga means that your approach/content needs to be different from all the other yoga books. Even if your book is well written and researched, why would they want a repeat of what has already been said?)

So, no chopping off of ears. Rather, listen to the feedback galleries give you when you do manage to get through the door. And keep on exploring new directions with your art. Dig deep within yourself until you find the unique expression that is you.

Artworks = income?

Q: *How many paintings/artworks do I need to have in the marketplace to be viable from an income perspective?*

A: Anthony has just had a solo exhibition, where the gallery requested 30 works. Doing these has meant other galleries now want work and he has no work to offer them, because it's all tied up. If the exhibition is a success then that's fabulous but, if not, he will have lost sales at his other galleries.

I've created a formula that works for me. Obviously it's not cast in stone and will vary depending on the popularity of the artist, but I work with an average return factor of 10% of the consigned value of the work. So for instance if you have £100,000 pounds' worth of consigned work in the marketplace, personally I'd expect an average monthly return of £10,000. In summer that'll rise to 20–30% but decrease to maybe only 5% in the winter months. This formula excludes special exhibitions. The point is, if you have £10,000 worth of work in total consigned in galleries, it's unlikely that you'll be earning £5000 a month. Seems obvious, but many artists are afraid to have too much consigned work – they want everything to sell as it's completed.

Different artists will experience different returns on their work on average, but it does give you an idea of the amount of work you need to expect a certain return. It goes without saying that, as you become more known, the return rate will increase, although outside factors such as recession/seasons can affect this. It may mean also that initially you'll have to work hard to build up a volume of work before you are able to just 'top up' galleries when sales occur.

Vanity insanity

Q: *Have you ever got an email asking to publish your work in an art book?*

A: I receive such emails regularly. The 'investment' varies but is usually around £1000 depending on how many pages I require. There's often a theme or title 'Modern Art Masters'. There is also much talk of distribution and often a 'selection' process (I select you when your cash hits my account I can't help feeling!). Doing the numbers, 100 artists would give the 'publishers' a gross income of £100, 000. Not bad, you'll agree, for putting a book together and clearly it must be working as they keep bringing out more books. Maybe it will be useful and add credibility to your work, if clients see it in a flashy looking book. I remain unconvinced. My questions would be:

- How many artists are you intending to cover?

- If, say, 500 and you are printing 2000 copies and giving away 2 to each artist that leaves only 1000 for distribution – not a great investment in terms of potential buyers from my perspective.

- What space will be allocated to each artist? A page? A chapter? Two column centimetres?

- What credibility will the publication have? Will it be introduced by a respected art critic for example?

- If I am a seriously bad artist can I still be accepted? In which case perhaps being associated with me will be detrimental to other better artists.

- Check to see if they are both the publisher and the distributor. Does this mean that they have agents countrywide as bigger distributors have? Otherwise how will they have the infrastructure to cover all the outlets in the country?

- What type of publicity/promotion and media do they have planned?

- Check out the publishing date. If it's vague such as: 'towards the end of the year' they could get your money and then you could wait for years before your book is published. Ask for a specific date by which your money will be returned in full if the book is not actually printed.

Getting work into galleries

Q: *How do I get work into galleries when they only are prepared to see emailed images and not the real work?*

A: The reason most galleries don't want to see you one to one initially, is:

- The time involved – most galleries get many requests a week and simply can't see each artist as they simply don't have the time. Emailed images or CD presentations are much faster to scan through and see if the work may be in the genre they are looking for or like. Some galleries get 20+ artists' requests a week. At 30 minutes a person, that's an extra day and a half per week added to their workload. So a screening procedure is usually favoured.

- It's easier emotionally to say 'no' in an email than face to face. It's less personal and they don't have angry/weeping artist to contend with.

It's just like the writing world where books are rejected with only a brief synopsis having been read and not the actual book. I've found that if one gallery which is respected has your work, then others are more receptive, valuing the other galleries' choice. This can work against you sometimes though as curators want work that is not available elsewhere.

Dangling a carrot may work, such as 'to date in my private capacity I have sold xx works, so I know there is a market out there for my work'. This may tempt a gallery to look further (provided of course that you have sold an impressive amount of work).

You can try a different approach so your email stands out from the rest of the applicants. You're creative, so think up a fresh approach that will intrigue/astound them. It may not work every time but at least you'll stand out from all the 'Hi my name is Susan and I'm an artist and here are some examples of my work . . . yawn'.

Failing stalking the owners (not recommended), that's about the best advice I can offer.

Bugs and beetles

The subject of beetles in stretchers had never occurred in our artistic lives, until a few weeks ago, when I went to a well-known gallery to swap a couple of works around. The gallery owner casually mentioned there had been a 'problem' with some works in his gallery.

I thought no more of it until I returned home and noticed ominous-looking holes in the stretchers of the two paintings. I called the gallery owner who assured me the paintings had been fumigated in a room specially constructed for the job. Another artist had apparently brought works into the gallery that had the beetles and they had infected all other stretchers made of similar wood. I don't feel I can sell the works holes *et al*, so will have to restretch the canvases on new stretchers. (I did consider a sheep barbeque using the 'sheep' paintings as both lamb and wood, but perhaps the wine had taken its toll at this point . . .) The point remains though, was the gallery liable for restretching of my work? Or is it just an act of nature, so no liability on the gallery's part? I have a good relationship with the gallery so did not force them to replace, but it is something to consider when consigning work in. A clause stating that the gallery is responsible may help but it would be hard to prove 100% that the beetles were not there before.

I have also been told by an entomologist that if the beetles breed in a certain variety of timber, they will not infect different wood but stick to the one they have chosen. I have changed the wood type in my stretchers and have had no further problems.

Contact details

Join the online art community

You're invited to join Ann and Anthony's art circle, 'Live Inspired', where you can:

- Post your experiences as an artist;

- Interact with other like minded souls;

- Read up about their experiences;

- Share information about the art world;

- Get feedback on galleries;

- Post questions about your art.

Become a member now by logging on to http://makingyourartwork. blogspot.com/

References

Cameron, J. (2011) *The Artist's Way: A Course in Discovering and Recovering Your Creative Self.* Houndsmills: Pan.

Clymo, R. (2007) *Create Your Own Website.* Harlow: Pearson Education Limited.

Grant, D. (2000) *The Business of Being an Artist.* New York: Allworth Press.

Grosenick, U. (2001) *Women Artists.* Italy: Taschen.

Hawkins, D.R. (2002) *Power vs. Force.* Carlsbad: Hay House.

Jassin, L.J. and Schechter, S.C. (1998) *The Copyright Permission and Libel Handbook.* New York: John Wiley & Sons.

Levison, J.C. (2007) *Guerrilla Marketing: Cutting-edge Strategies for the 21st Century.* London: Piatkus.

Marshall, I. and Zohar, D. (2004) *Spiritual Capital: Wealth We Can Live By.* London: Bloomsbury.

Michells, C. (2001) *How to Survive and Prosper as an Artist.* New York: Henry Holt and Company.

Mostert, F. and Apolzon, L.E. (2007) *From Edison to iPod.* London: Dorling Kindersley.

Saatchi, C. (2008) *My Name is Charles Saatchi and I'm an Artoholic.* London: Phaidon Press Ltd.

Stout, M. (2007) *The Sociopath Next Door.* New York: Bantam Doubleday.

Tolle, E. (2001) *The Power of Now: A Guide to Spiritual Enlightenment.* London: Hodder.

Zohar, D. and Marshall, I. (2004) *Spiritual Capital – Wealth We Can Live By.* London: Bloomsbury.

Index